# DHARMA vs.
# ADHARMA

*PART-1*

# THE VICIOUS PROPAGANDA AGAINST JAT RESERVATION

*"Yadrishi Bhavana Yasya, Siddhir Bhavati Tadrishi"*

## About the Book

Falsehood, ill will, covetousness and defamation are the tools of Hype (Adharma). This book, **Nyaya Dharma (Ethics of Justice)** is part 1 of the two-part book **Yato-Dharmasto-Jaya**, to present the conflicts between Truth (Dharma) and Hype (Adharma) by displaying the vicious propaganda (hype) carried out by forces of Adharma like media, institutions and ideological (conditioned) minds in support of a decision which should not have been taken at the first instance and even if taken should have been opposed by right-minded or people with considerations for Dharma.

66

*"Nothing is higher than dharma. The weak overcomes the stronger by dharma, as over a king. Truly that dharma is the truth (Satya). Therefore, when a man speaks the truth, they say, "He speaks the Dharma, and if he speaks dharma they say, "he speaks the truth." For both are one.*

-By Sage Yajnavalkya (Brihadaranyaka Upanishad)

99

# Disclaimer

Whatever is written in this book regarding Jat Reservation is based on the objective and rational interpretation of the facts and the legal principles used in Writ Petition Civil- 274 of 2014. The content of the book is already given in the Supreme Court of India through a Writ Petition. Only when the petition was rejected on trivial matters, without giving an opportunity to present my case that I decided to present the truth behind the Hype created by the vested interests against Jat Reservation. I hope after reading the book people you will feel that whatever is written in the book is the need of dharma.

## Dedication

*This book is dedicated to Lord Ram, Mata Sita and My Deity for making dharma clear to me and guiding me to work for the cause of Dharma*

# Preface

The battle between Dharma (truth) and Adharma (hype) is always the battle between the objectivity (with a basis in knowledge) and subjectivity (with a basis in ignorance). The increasing crimes of the society with their changing nature or the diminishing values among individuals, all are symptoms of the increase in Adharma.

This increase in Adharma or the decreasing Dharma is not because of a lack of people or institutions to protect Dharma. But it is lack of awareness on Dharma with an active propagation and support to Adharma by people and institutions, either through intentional ignorance or unintentional ignorance. Therefore, it becomes a necessity for an Arya (Aryan) to make Dharma clear to them and helps the world in its development as a noble place to live.

This book (**Part 1** of **Yato-Dharmasto-Jaya**) focuses on Adharma and displays how vicious the Adharma is in its approach. The intentional and unintentional ignorance are the tools of this defective approach adopted by Adharma. We will capture the same through the most obnoxious judgment of our time i.e. cancellation of Jat Reservation. It was one such exercise of subjective interpretation of the facts or the ignorance of common universal principles and facts by responsible institutions and a collusion of interest groups like National Commission of Backward Classes (NCBC), media etc., a display of the presence of Adharma at some of the highest positions.

But, the establishment of dharma in the world is not something which can be done just by pointing Adharma. Establishment of Dharma requires more than just the exercise of finding faults in the people on the side of Adharma. Formation of a society based on Dharma requires conscious and constructive efforts of an Arya to create inclination of people towards Dharma or Righteousness. Thousands of year ago it was Lord Ram who guided the people towards Dharma and people displayed moral attitude for the establishment of a Dharma based society. Today, with the grace of my idols, I will try to repeat the same message in Part-II of the book "**Yato-Dharmasto-Jaya**".

While learning and understanding Dharma, we can't overlook the irresponsible forces of Adharma. We need an objective and rational mindset to understand both and promote one. Our focus should be equally distributed towards the establishment of Dharma and on removing the false and fabricated notions of Adharma.

Therefore, before discussing Dharma it becomes important for us to talk in detail about Adharma (the point of discussion in this book). In this, we will discuss- how the lack of comprehensiveness leads to Adharma; by dismantling the very tools of hype (Adharma) - like falsehood, ill will, covetousness and defamation.

In the second book, we will focus on the understanding of Dharma by revisiting the important laws of nature, as Lord Ram said,

**"The will of God is expressed through the laws of Nature"**

## Introduction to Nyaya Dharma

This book, **Nyaya Dharma (Ethics of Justice)** is based on the objective analysis of NCBC report on Jat Reservation and Supreme Court of India judgment in Writ Petition Civil- 274 of 2014, as it is not just a judgment against which I have gone to the Highest Court but it is also a case where the forces of Adharma were far more visible with all its major ancillaries working in support of each other.

The book is designed in steps and a flow where any person who is well-versed in law or Nyaya Dharma, the reading of Chapter 1 of the book is good enough for them to summarily reject the Supreme Court Judgment. It presents enough reasons to agree with the future ideas and understand the falsehood and covetousness used by the forces of Adharma.

The written laws suggest that the moment we show the presence of imputed bias, the decision of the judge becomes void without the need for an investigation into the likelihood or suspicion of bias. But because of high subjectivity in the interpretation of laws with lack of moral attitude among the forces of Adharma, the law in practice has differed a lot from the written laws. The forces of Adharma have remained adamant to uphold their biases and the hate against the Jat community by putting a Clock of Notional Justice over their hate.

Others who might have some stronger resistances or influences of Adharma, might be able to overcome those resistance by the end of this book, as by the end of the book we will not just expose the forces of Adharma but we will also understand why the NCBC Report which Supreme Court accepted as having enough reasons to give Judgment against Jat Reservation was nothing more than an imaginary and biased report.

This ill will and covetousness among the forces of Adharma has forced me to carry out a detailed analysis of the NCBC report and the functioning of many organizations set for specific moral attitudes, like National Legal Services Authority of India (NALSA), Supreme Court Legal Services Committee (SCLSC) and National Human Rights Commission of India (NHRC), but becoming stalled or disoriented from that cause. It is our misfortune that we have activists of cause instead of rational and objective people manning these institutions.

Still, if someone is having a strongly conditioned mind or follows some blind ideologies, I will try to make everything crystal clear to them through the Part II **'Dharma'** of the book **'Yato-Dharmasto-Jaya'**.

The uncovering of the vicious propaganda against Jat Reservation is just the tip of the iceberg in understanding the actual nature of the forces of Adharma. Being the best representative of Vedic Aryan (from the perspective of Supreme Court of India), the same clan to which Lord Ram belonged, it is my sacrosanct duty to work towards the cause of Dharma and clear the Adharma present in our environment, as one of our ancient ideas say:

*"Yadrishi Bhavana Yasya, Siddhir Bhavati Tadrishi"*

*i.e.*

**"Whatever are one's thoughts, so will be the outcome. Our thoughts are influenced by our environment. Hence we need to clean our environment."**

# Table of Contents

Actual Bias: The Foundations of the Supreme Court of India Judgment

## ॐ 6 (Chapter)

### Jat Reservation and the Pathetic Media

How Bogus Media tries to Manipulate Opinions

## ॐ 7 (Chapter)

### The Added Responsibilities on Court

Ending the Intrigue Work against Dharma

**Epilogue**

References with Links to Supreme Court Judgment, NCBC report etc.

http://www.ncbc.nic.in/Writereaddata/Supreme%20Court%20Judgement-2015%20Jat%20Caste635647145288159656.pdf

http://www.ncbc.nic.in/Writereaddata/JAT%202014635568274253868064.pdf

http://www.indialegallive.com/constitutional-law-news/special-report-news/supreme-court-on-jat-reservation-muscle-flexing-reaps-nothing-46123

https://thewire.in/politics/the-absurdity-of-jat-reservation

https://www.lawnotes.in/Principles_of_Natural_Justice

http://www.legalservicesindia.com/article/1519/Principles-of-Natural-Justice-In-Indian-Constitution.html

https://en.wikipedia.org/wiki/Natural_justice

Principles of Natural Justice by Justice Brijesh Kumar (http://ijtr.nic.in/articles/art36.pdf)

http://www.lawvedic.com/article/principles-of-natural-justice-in-indian-constitution-177

Dysfunctional Institutions? Towards a New Agenda in Governance Studies (http://faculty.washington.edu/aseem/R&G.pdf)

https://indianexpress.com/article/india/india-news-india/govt-questions-obc-status-of-many-in-upsc-list-backward-panel-warns-of-stir-2956919/

https://economictimes.indiatimes.com/news/politics-and-nation/obc-panel-opposes-dopt-sacking-of-120-employees/articleshow/53549409.cms

# ॐ 1

## The Principle of Natural Justice

**The Reason Enough to Make Supreme Court Judgment Null & Void**

*Indeed, natural justice is a pervasive facet of secular law where a spiritual touch enlivens legislation, administration and adjudication, to make fairness a creed of life. It has many colours and shades, many forms and shapes and, save where valid law excludes, it applies when people are affected by acts of authority. It is the bone of healthy government, recognised from earliest times and not a mystic testament of judge-made law. Indeed from the legendary days of Adam- and of Kautilya's Arthashastra-the rule of law has had this stamp of natural justice, which makes it social justice. We need not go into these deeps for the present except to indicate that the roots of natural justice and its foliage are noble and not new-fangled. Today its application must be sustained by current legislation, case law or other extant principle, not the hoary chords of legend and history. Our jurisprudence has sanctioned its prevalence even like the Anglo-American system.*

> - Supreme Court of India in Mohinder Singh Gill v. Chief Election Commissioner, AIR 1978 SC 851

## Introduction

In the eyes of Law, Principle of Natural Justice is as essential as any other principle to the cause of Justice. The Principle of Natural Justice brings fairness in decisions, helping judiciary in earning confidence and trust of ordinary people. But as a principle it was not explicitly mentioned in the Indian Constitution, requiring active interventions from Indian Judiciary to make it an essential part of modern-day justice delivery system of India.

Today, its importance can be realized from the fact that this principle has become fundamental to the protection of human rights by serving as the foundation for equity and equality among all. Equity and equality brings fairness not just in the social and economical activities of the people but also acts as a shield for the protection of individual liberty against the arbitrary action of authorities.

The Principle of Natural Justice serves the court in an unequivocal manner as a procedural principle, helping not just in decision-making but also in the development of other principles. Therefore, we can say that under the present time it is a necessity to be taken into consideration by every judicial, quasi-judicial and administrative agency before taking any decision that adversely affects the rights of a private individuals or group of people. And when this principle is overlooked deliberately or in ignorance and the judiciary shows no will to correct itself when pointed out to it, we are left with no option but to touch the conscience of each individual against the ideologies and biases existing in the judiciary.

But before we move forward on our discussion, we need to know about two critical things-

1. What exactly principle of Natural Justice means? and

2. Why principle of Natural Justice is so important that it can hold the Supreme Court Judgment as void.

Therefore, before going about the violations of the principle of Natural Justice by the judges of Supreme Court of India we will answer these questions first.

## What is principle of Natural Justice?

The principle of Natural Justice, also known as *common-sense justice*, is a technical term pointing to two major ideas, as:

a) **Nemo Iudex in Causa Sua**, a Latin phrase meaning *"No one should be a Judge of his own cause"* or the rule against bias, and

b) **Audi Alteram Partem**, another Latin phrase meaning *"Let the other side be heard as well"* or the right to fair hearing.

In brief, the first idea of rule against bias helps the justice delivery system by keeping the vested interests away from decision-making and the second idea of right to fair hearing helps justice delivery system in knowing the perspectives of both sides before making a decision.

For our discussion in this chapter, I will focus on the First major idea i.e. **Nemo Iudex in Causa Sua**, using the Supreme Court of India decision on Writ Petition Civil **274 of 2014** as the allegory to display the violations of this idea of the principle of Natural Justice, the idea which is an essential part of the human rights and fundamental to justice delivery by court.

## Why Natural Justice?

Before we learn more about the idea of Nemo Iudex in Causa Sua and how it was violated in the Writ petition Civil 274 of 2014, we must learn about the importance of rule against bias in the functioning of the judicial and administrative system of any nation and why it is essential in the kind of diverse society we have.

Historically, India had a social way of living which was based on collectivism. That collectivism served as the basis of our unity in diversity. That unity is visible in the shared history and culture where almost everyone had an important role and had dependence on each other.

Today, that collectivism is fast replaced by the individualism, with the judicial and political agencies acting as the institutions to promote and preserve that individualism. This increased individualism in India, a copy from the western nations and the need of modern-day economy, has lead to the formation of hundreds of interest groups in the public and private spaces of India.

The limited resources of the nation and the desire to have control over the maximum resources among different groups have made these interests groups visible across India. In every election whether it is politicians or the media all talks and promotes those interests groups and show the importance of each interest group in political calculations. In addition to that we have additional added qualifications to make it tough for some and ease it for some.

Under such circumstances, if the functions of national institutions like courts are not charged in a just and fair manner the **Rule of Law** loses its validity. These lose of validity causes the erosion of public confidence in the judiciary, undermining the nobility of the legal system and leads to ensuing chaos. Any violation of natural justice leads to arbitrariness, an act against the equality before law.

In fact, the very first fundamental principle of the Rule of Law and our constitution on Fundamental rights is to have Equality before Law. Therefore, despite no explicit mention of the principle of Natural Justice in Indian Constitution, Supreme Court of India being the interpreter of the Constitution has firmly grounded the principle of Natural Justice to Article 14 and 21 of Indian Constitution.

**Article 14** of the Indian Constitution i.e. **Equality Before Law** states that- *The State shall not deny to any person equality before the law or the equal protection of the laws within the territory of India.*

Equality is antithetical to arbitrariness. Equality is a part of true democracy, a sign of Rule of Law where all people have same rights and same opportunities to grow and prosper. Whereas arbitrariness is a part of Anarchy, sign of Matsya Nyaya i.e. Law of Fish or the Law of Jungle where power defines the rule. Therefore, to ensure fairness and equality towards all and nullify the arbitrary actions of the State, principle of Natural Justice becomes essential.

The principle of Natural Justice ensures that the actions of State must be based on valid and relevant principles which can be applied alike to all people or groups which are similarly situated. No extraneous or irrelevant consideration should be used to deny the equality before law.

*Mala fide exercise of power and arbitrariness are different lethal radiations emanating from the same vice: in fact the latter comprehends the former. Both are inhibited by Articles 14 and 16."* (**Justice J Bhagwati of Supreme Court of India in E. P. Royappa vs State Of Tamil Nadu & Anr on 23 November, 1973**)

Now, the questions immediately arises out of it is- What is the requirement of Article 14? What is the content and reach of the great equalizing principle enunciated in this article?

Before Writ Petition Civil 274 of 2014 Supreme Court never had doubt that equality is the founding faith of the Constitution, the pillar on which the foundations of our democratic republic rests securely. In words of Supreme Court, Equality must not be subjected to a narrow, pedantic or lexicographic approach. No attempt should be made to truncate its all-embracing scope and meaning, for to do so would be to violate its activist magnitude.

**Now Consider this from NCBC report (Page No. 116 of report/Page No. 118 of pdf link on NCBC report)**

(a)    Apart from Justice K.C. Gupta, the other Members of the Commission were Shri Jai Singh Bishnoi, Shri Som Dutt, Advocate, Shri Arjun Dev Gulati, Shri Rao Ranpal Singh and Shri Telu Ram Jangra. It is seen that Shri Bishnoi belongs to Bishnoi caste and Shri Som Dutt is a Ror. In other words, in the Commission, two of the Members had interests in the outcome of the case since Bishnoi and Ror castes were under consideration and thus the composition was not following one of the cardinal principals of Natural Justice which says - "Nemo Judex In Re Sua". A man shall not be judge in his own cause. The Report gave OBC status (albeit "Special") to Rors and Bishnois along with three other castes including Jats. Speaker after speaker after gave vent to this allegation of bias during the Public Hearing.

(b) Not only this, it is also seen that the report of the Justice K.C Gupta Commission was primarily based on the survey conducted in the year 2012 by the MDU, Rohtak. The project was implemented by the single Project Director, a retired Prof. K.S. Sangwan. Incidentally, he is also belonging to the Jat community. The Vice Chancellor of the MDU, Rohtak during the concerned period was Prof. R.P. Hooda who is also a Jat. All of them were accused of bias in the whole survey and subsequent report during the Public Hearings held in Delhi.

(vi)   The survey was conducted among 49,817 households belonging to 16 castes drawn from all the Districts of Haryana. Interestingly, the comparable figures for Ahirs, Yadavas, Kurmis and Gujars (which are otherwise said to be comparable OBC communities) have not been studied for any of the Social, Educational or Economic parameters either in the MDU Report or in the Commission's report. During the Public Hearing, many presenters pointed this out that if they are compared with these groups, the Jats will be seen to be superior. The Survey compared the Jats mostly with higher castes like Bhramins, Rajputs, Punjabis, Vaish, Gaur etc which are in any case higher classes.

If having Jat, Bishnoi or Ror Community members as part of the commission violates **Nemo Judex in Re Sua** on the members of the NCBC Commission.

# NATIONAL COMMISSION FOR BACKWARD CLASSES

Hon'ble Shri Justice V. Eswaraiah, Chairperson

Hon'ble Shri S. K. Kharventhan, Member

Hon'ble Shri A. K. Saini, Member

Hon'ble Shri A. K. Mangotra, Member Secretary

- How many names in the list belongs to the existing OBC list? Or increase the scope of these observations:
  - To which community B P Mandal belonged that his report was not in violation of the Nemo Judex in Re Sua?
  - To which community does most of the members of the commissions like National Commission for Scheduled Castes, National Commission for Scheduled Tribes, National Commission for Minorities or the Members of the National Commission for Religious and Linguistics Minorities under an ex-Supreme Court Judge (popularly known as Ranganath Mishra Commission) belonged that the principle of **"Nemo Judex in Re Sua"** was not violated by them.

Such discriminatory views of NCBC and other organizations/people against the Jat Reservation are very well answered by Supreme Court of India itself long back in **S.G. Jaisinghani v. Union of India, (1967) 2 SCR 703:**

*"It is important to emphasize that the absence of arbitrary power is the first essential of the rule of law upon which our whole constitutional system is based. In a system governed by rule of law, discretion, when conferred upon executive authorities, must be confined within clearly defined limits. The rule of law from this point of view means that decisions should be made by the application of known principles and rules and, in general, such decisions should be predictable and the citizen*

*should know where he is. If a decision is taken without any principle or without any rule it is unpredictable and such a decision is the antithesis of a decision taken in accordance with the rule of law.*

This observation from Supreme Court leads us to ask two relevant questions:

- **When from Commissions working under retired Judges or Committees set under the Supreme Court Judges all had and even today have members from the same community, Were the observations of NCBC confined to the clearly defined limits or precedence's followed?**

- **Was the application of known principles and rules by NCBC is predictable and Jat or any other community can guess where they are?**

According to the set precedence's of the Supreme Court, Rule of Law is a sworn enemy of Caprice. The tacit support to the caprices by the responsible authorities has exposed the vagaries present in the Rule of Law. The NCBC report was in violation of the Rule of Law or the Equality before Law and it was the duty of the Supreme Court of India to declare such report as null and void.

In words of **Justice Douglas, United States v. Wunderlick [342 US 98] (1951)**, "Law has reached its finest moments when it has freed man from the unlimited discretion of some ruler, some civil or military official, some bureaucrat. Where discretion, is absolute, man has always suffered. At times, it has been his property that has been invaded; at times, his privacy; at times, his liberty of movement; at times, his freedom of thought; at times, his life. Absolute discretion is a ruthless master. It is more destructive of freedom than any of man's other inventions."

Despite the clear set precedence, NCBC report was accepted by the Judges of the Supreme Court and presented as a well researched report and made it mandatory for the Government to follow, Why?

Because we have people who try to hide their hate, biases, interests or ignorance by putting the clock of justice over them. Here we will discuss about the imputed bias of the Judge considered as the architect of the judgment. When each professor, member or any other person belonging to Jat community is a biased personality, what on earth can make us believe that others were not biased towards their interest.

The lies of NCBC report has shown how deep their biases are and how much bigger lies were made by the members of present OBC community in the representations made against the Jat reservation. Under such conditions having a Judge who himself belonged to the OBC community, (AHOM community- the first Entry from the State of Assam in the Central List of OBCs for the State of Assam by Resolution No. 12011/68/93-BCC(C) dt 10/09/1993), whole exercise becomes an exercise carried in bad faith and Principle of Natural Justice is the sworn enemy of such malafide intentions.

The very first act of having a Judge from OBC Community in the Jat Reservation case was in violation of the set legal precedents and in violation of the principle of Natural Justice, making the whole judgment **null and void.** But before seeking some more information on that we should seek answer to the important question that- Can a Supreme Court of India Judge be biased?

The things which I have observed in many judgments of the Supreme Court and the interactions which I had with the Supreme Court Judges, my friends or people with legal knowledge, One thing which is abundantly clear is that we have Judges in our legal system who are guided by the ideologies and the biases, rather than dharma.

This was verified by the four-most senior judges of the Supreme Court of India (after CJI in terms of work experience in Supreme Court) who came out in open against CJI in January 2018 and made a press conference that many cases are given to judges who passed favorable judgments'. When all legal definitions are same, provisions are same then how can the judgments' vary? The answer is the ideologies and interests who define the position of a Judge and the judge interpret the laws and precedents based on those interests.

Though the four judges gained nothing from their exercise but the four judges told the world that in Indian Judiciary we have observations beyond the written laws and set legal precedence's, giving a space for varied interpretations. Based on our observations, opinions and ideologies the judgment would have differed from the present judgment, showing that the Judges are often in violation of the impartiality.

**Impartiality**, a feature of decision-making whose essence in law was rightfully observed by **Lord Denning, the Master of the Rolls, in *Metropolitan Properties Co (FGC) Ltd v Lannon* (1968)**:

*"Justice must be rooted in confidence and confidence is destroyed when right-minded people go away thinking: 'The judge was biased."*

*Or*

What **Lord Hewart, the Lord Chief Justice of England and Wales** had to say on Public confidence as the basis for the rule against bias *"it is not merely of some importance, but of fundamental importance that justice should not only be done, but should manifestly be seen to be done."*

In legal system we have three kind of bias under the **Nemo Iudex in Causa Sua** or under the **rule against bias**, as:

1. Actual Bias,

2. Imputed Bias, and

3. Apparent Bias.

The first kind of bias i.e. **Actual Bias** is the kind of bias where the decision-maker was prejudiced in favor of or against a party. The second kind of bias i.e. **Imputed Bias** is a kind of situation where the decision-maker being a party to a suit, or having a pecuniary or proprietary interest in the outcome of the decision. And the third kind of bias i.e. **Apparent Bias** is the kind of bias where a judge or other decision-maker is not a party to a matter and does not have an interest in its outcome, but through his or her conduct or behavior gives rise to a suspicion that he or she is not impartial.

If we read about our history, we will find that it was always one or another form of biases prevalent in the decision-makers or the forces of Adharma which threatened the cause of Dharma every time and forced the Dharma to prove its existence. In **Ramayana**, it was the biased attitude of Ravana which never recognized the faults of his Sister Surpanakha, or in **Mahabharata** we had the biases of Dhritarashtra towards his son leading to a war between Dharma and Adharma.

The judgment for Cancellation of Jat Reservation was also one such biased exercise where we had all the three forms of biases present together. However, the people who are in legal practice think that, the making of the allegations of Actual Bias is very rare as it is very hard to prove. Therefore, for the sake of brevity I have pointed out only the Imputed Bias of the decision-makers and the Actual and Apparent Bias are reserved for the discussion on NCBC Report to show that even the bases of the Judgment were nothing but a biased report.

## How this principle makes Supreme Court Judgment Null & Void?

If we speak legally then the presence of Imputed Bias like any other bias is a violation of the idea of **Nemo Iudex in Causa Sua,** an irrefutable fact of law where the disqualification becomes automatic and the decision-maker is barred from adjudicating the matter without the need for any investigation into the likelihood or suspicion of bias.

The classic case on Imputed Bias is the case of **Dimes v Grand Junction Canal (1852)**, where Lord Cottenham was disqualified from deciding the case without an inquiry because of the pecuniary interests of the Judge. If we talk about personal interests, we have the unprecedented case of **R v Bow Street Metropolitan Stipendiary Magistrate Ex parte Pinochet Ugarte (No.2) (1999)** where Lord Hoffmann was disqualified from the case and the outcome of proceedings were set aside by the Law Lords, because of the close connection of Judge with one of the party.

From the above cases we can make out that a person is barred from deciding any case in which he or she may be, or may fairly be suspected to be, biased. Removing biases is the need of impartiality and it applies to all courts of law, tribunals, arbitrators or anyone having the duty to act judicially. In a nation where highest political office holders use community identities to gain votes it becomes an added responsibility on the courts to avoid such incidents in the courts to maintain the public confidence in the legal system.

The increasing dominance of manmade laws over the laws of nature has created open seas of interpretation for decision-makers. Under such conditions, the principle of Natural Justice, being based on good conscience and human values, brings equity and equality in the judicial system through a fair procedure. Procedure, where deciding authority acts in an impartial and unbiased manner. Having an impartial decision-maker is a matter of faith, which a common man must have, in the deciding authority.

*Since, natural justice is a pervasive facet of secular law and fairness, the open violations of the principle of natural justice shows that we are living in an unsecular society with biases as a creed of life. Where an unhealthy government rules over people and judges make their own laws. In words of **Lord Mansfield, John Wilkes [(1770) 4 Burr. 2528 at 2539]**, "Discretion means sound* *discretion guided by law. It must be governed by rule, not by humor; it must not be arbitrary, vague, and fanciful".*

*The decision on cancellation of Jat Reservation has undermined the nobility of the legal system and the ensuing chaos in Haryana was a live example of this. Our Constitution through the social and economic justice aspirations in the preamble and through the Right to Equality and Life puts an obligation on the Supreme Court to perform its constitutional responsibilities under Article 32 in a fair and impartial manner.*

*I hope and pray that the court will take cognizance of the violations on its part against the cause of Dharma and it will correct its actions which were against its own motto of 'Yato-Dharmasto-Jaya.'*

ॐ 2

## Initial steps of my Legal Fight

**T**he **S**talled **I**nstitutions **(NALSA, SCLSC** and **NHRC)** of our **D**emocracy

*Having a moral attitude is a wonderful thing. It gives a reason to the life and pushes a person to work for that reason. History tells us that all people, whether famous or infamous, are remembered for the cause they served. The functions and festivals we celebrate every year are just a remembrance of the victory of goodness and truthfulness over the evil and false. In our so called more civilized and educated world we requires dedicated institutions to preserve and serve some of those essential moral attitudes like Human Rights, Justice etc. But in all those pious thoughts of moral attitude we failed to realize that people have personal morals.*

*Today, we have institutions but the functioning of these institutions is surrendered to the freewill of few. These institutions respond only when the cause of moral attitude is in line to personal beliefs or own notions of moral attitude. This use of ignorant freewill against the moral attitude by institutions makes us wonder- What kind of institutions we have established? Are they serving the cause for which they were established or the people serving in those institutions have identified own causes to serve? Whether this runaway from the defined causes stalls the progression of moral attitude for which they were established?*

## Introduction

Nearly a century ago, Oscar Wilde, a famous Irish Poet and Playwright, said:

**"Morality is simply the attitude we adopt towards people whom we personally dislike"**

The observation of Oscar Wilde seems very true in our world where almost every day we observe such attitudes. People who support one political party or leader will question other political parties or leaders on some practices while justifying the same practices from the person or party of liking as political compulsions. The champions of Freedom of Expression will work hard to suppress the ideas of others.

Or the people from media, scholars, NGOs and other institutions who are very happy to identify themselves with the groups based on profession, workplace, intellect, interests, color and region will start questioning the people who identify themselves through biological inheritance i.e. Jati, as irrational and narrow minded people.

When people with such perspectives starts governing the institutions established for the cause of a moral attitude the institution starts moving away from the cause for which it was established and takes to the path of becoming a dysfunctional or turning into an interest-based group rather than serving the cause of moral attitude for which it is established. These people are the people about whom Oscar Wilde talked, as they makes it seem real that morality has become an attitude towards people of dislike.

The same subjective moralities were encountered by me when I started my journey against the forces of Adharma. While I have detailed some of those here but I sincerely believe that these errors of subjective morality are caused by the lack of knowledge on Dharma. These subjective moralities dominates our way of thinking, our perspectives and our understanding of the right and wrong as long as we are influenced by the forces of Adharma.

## My First Letter to NALSA (National Legal Services Authority of India)

Many people, while cherishing the NCBC report against Jat Reservation and Supreme Court of India judgment as some kind of path-breaking judgment, are yet to realize that the above exercise proved nothing more clearly than to tacitly accept that Jat is the best representative of Vedic Arya. The community to which Lord Ram belonged, making them the rightful inheritors of the Lord Ram.

So, in July 2016, I wrote a letter to the Hon'ble Chief Justice of India and his Lordship's Companion Justices of the Supreme Court of India that as courts have accepted that Jat is the best Vedic Aryan, so what on earth can keep the interests of

Jat away from Ram Janmabhoomi. Under Article 21 of the constitution only Jat has the Right to Inheritance for the land.

Copies of that letter were also forwarded to the Patron-in-Chief, NALSA (The Chief Justice of India) and the Executive Chief of NALSA to provide legal assistance through NALSA with listing of matter as Public Interest Litigation (PIL) for the protection of the Fundamental Rights of Vedic Arya community.

Article 21 of the Constitution of India, also known as the Right to Life guarantees every Citizen of India to have Right to Livelihood. The Right to Livelihood includes Right to Succession or Inheritance, so the land of a Vedic Aryan should be handed over to Vedic Aryan only.

The works done by Lord Ram towards the establishment of Vedic Dharma and the salutations used in Ramayana for Lord Ram proves it beyond doubt that Ram was an Aryan. And we have some beautiful lines by Valmiki, used for Ram as:

**"Arya Sarva Samascaiva Sadaiva Priyadarsanah"**

**I.e., an Arya, who worked for the equality of all and was dear to anyone**

## The Choosy Institution of NALSA

NALSA was established in December 1995 as an Institution to provide free legal support to eligible people and serve the cause of Justice. As a person with no job, leading to my income below 1lakh I was entitled to have NALSA help. So, I sent a copy of the letter which I sent to Judges/Registrar with request to give legal aid.

A month passed without having a response from NALSA. While NALSA boasts itself as an institution to provide 'Access to Justice for All' but all those ideals become irrelevant when they are required to work against their ideologies. This forced me to write an email to SCLSC in August 2016 with a copy to

NALSA detailing about my letter and the inaction on the part of NALSA.

In a day or two of my email, I received a letter from UNDER SECRETARY, NALSA regarding the representation for Legal Assistance. The Under Secretary told that he is directed to inform me that as per Regulation 14(6) of the Supreme Court Legal Services Committee Regulations 1996, the Supreme Court Legal Services Committee does not provide legal services inter alia to a person who is concerned with the proceedings only in a representative or official capacity.

Let's look at the conclusions which can be drawn from the whole incident:

1. My seeking of legal help was only in representative or in official capacity,

2. We have Legal Regulations which restrict the legal services offered by NALSA or the access to Justice and they can't be offered to a person only being a representative or in official capacity,

3. Either the Patron-in-Chief or the Executive Chief of NALSA forwarded the letter and likely directed the Under Secretary to give the above reply to my letter.

Before we look and explore these conclusions, let's look at the Regulation 14 and its part 14(6) of the Supreme Court Legal Services Committee Regulations 1996 which restricted my access to help from NALSA.

The Regulation 14 of the Supreme Court Legal Services Committee Regulations 1996 deals with the certain cases where Legal Services shall not be given by the NALSA. The best way for the validation of the above argument is to check the history of NALSA.

If we search for NALSA we will find the organization is popular for National Legal Services Authority vs. Union of India case where NALSA was the primary petitioner and it argued for the fundamental rights of the Transgender people. When NALSA can help transgender for fundamental rights why it can't support any other community like JAT?

In the above case it was not that whole community approached the NALSA. It must have been few individual, NGO etc. who have approached NALSA. The arguments of being a representative or in official capacity are excuses to create delusions with no observable precedent in the functioning of NALSA.

If we talk about the representative or official capacity, I would like to make it clear that according to Preamble of our Constitution we are a secular state and it is the duty of every structure of state, be it courts, executive or legislature, all have a duty to protect the freedom of thought, expression, belief, faith and worship of every individual. Even if I only say that I want to preserve and practice my Arya Dharma, it is the responsibility of every state organization to provide that freedom to me.

In addition to that, the same Supreme Court Legal Services Committee Regulations 1996 have Regulation 15, which provides for giving Legal Help irrespective of the means test in cases of great public importance. So, let's look at the great public importance of my matter.

*If we look at India and observe the History, Culture and Polity of India, everyone knows how important Lord Ram, Aryan way of life and Dharma is in it. Even Supreme Court of India carries the Aryan Ethical position of* **"Yato-Dharmasto-Jaya"** *as its motto. A normal citizen may overlook these facts but to believe that an organization working under Supreme Court with Supreme Court Judges as the main guiding force of NALSA it is more of strange limitations to the means test of the Regulation 14.*

In addition to that, the judges holds the power to convert the letter into PIL and when it comes to fundamental rights of citizens it becomes an added responsibility on judges to do so. When Supreme Court has identified that Jat are of Aryan identity, it becomes a duty on them and its affiliated organizations to protect the culture and way of life at least when requested to do so. It is not that NALSA is beyond the mandate of the constitution of India or the ideals and aspirations of it.

In reality the whole argument of NALSA was too vague to be digested for a reasonable person. And, I raised the issue with NALSA and SCLSC to reconsider their position because of no grounds to back it. I made it clear to them that as an Arya I don't feel that my request is just in representative or official capacity. My position is as much personal as anyone else on earth can have. To remove your vague criteria of representative or official capacity consider me as the only petitioner.

And, it is not that **NALSA** and **SCLSC** were not aware of their frivolous replies. I have seen them changing the online replies given on my issue at a later date to avoid future embarrassment or putting replies an year late to show that we considered the request. The later modifications are enough to show the biased ideologies of NALSA and SCLSC.

All this happens only because of the feeling of being secure from any action by top.

## My Petition and the delays

The ideologies of Courts, NALSA or any other organization are clear to me from day one but having evidences was important to show the actual bias. In parallel to other things, in October 2016 I filed a WRIT PETITION under Article 32 as petitioner-in-person.

It is open secret for every Indian that when it comes to matters of money and appreciation for their ideology we have extra-fast trials. For poor individuals or ideas against their ideology it becomes a painful ordeal of procedures, rules and times.

Nearly after two months of filling my petition and many calls I got a Dairy number for my case and made aware of the defects in my petition. Here comes another important observation:

*When it comes to the petitions in line with the ideologies it becomes immaterial to look for formats and procedures. When it comes to Dharma it requires the petition to be in proper format.*

As a person with not much knowledge on court formats, I managed to remove the defects in 24-25 days and again submitted the petitions. But I was not aware that even after fulfilling the needs of courts they have kept too much power to protect and uphold Adharma.

So, first they kept the petition on hold. Whenever I asked for the progress the file was either forwarded to authority or the PIL-Writ will say that your petition is with Writ Section. When I told them that Writ Section forwarded it to PIL-Writ, they will say ok we will look and respond soon.

## Requests to another stalled institution for Human Rights

Some of the conditions or responses which I mentioned as of now in the first chapter and above in this chapter showed acts by authorities were in violation of the Universal Declaration of Human Rights (UDHR) like violation of Right to Equality (Article 1), Freedom from Discrimination (Article 2), Right to Equality before Law (Article 7), Right to Remedy by Competent Tribunal (Article 8), Freedom of Belief and Religion (Article 18) etc.

So, I moved to National Human Rights Commission (NHRC) with the appeal that despite having a human right of Right to Remedy by Competent Tribunal, my petition has seen little or no progress in 4 months. NHRC have some standard replies which are used by them when someone's appeal is not according to the ideology they wish to promote. E.g. on my first complaint they said that:

On perusal of the complaint, it is seen that the complaint relates to the matter which is sub judice before a Court/Tribunal, hence the complaint is not entertainable by the Commission, as per Regulation 9(xi) of the N.H.R.C. (Procedure) Regulations, 1997. The complaint is filed and the case is closed.

And when I brought various articles of the Universal Declaration of Human Rights to my appeal, the reply became:

On perusal of the complaint, it is seen that the allegations do not make out any specific violation of human rights, hence the complaint is not entertainable by the Commission, as per Regulation 9(x) of the N.H.R.C. (Procedure) Regulations, 1997. The complaint is filed and the case is closed.

The replies of NHRC show that for them protection of Human Rights depend on the person in front. I had one more incident of NHRC where my Right to Fair Trial was compromised. But the subjective biases in them are so much that they can't come out of it.

## What it means to have such biased institutions

Institutions like NALSA, SCLSC or NHRC are established to protect the fundamental rights of each and every citizen. It is the basic moral attitude they are supposed to uphold and work for the promotion of it. Providing Legal help in the issues of protection of Fundamental Rights is the bare minimum to expect from them. By fulfilling these moral attitudes, institutions creates a win-win situation by meeting the expectations of people and helping in identification of permitted, prescribed, and prohibited actions from these institutions as well as to restrict the misuse by others.

The present acts of these institutions where they identify themselves with subjective morals and principles instead of the objective and universal moral attitudes, is the main reason of rising asymmetries of power and inequities. While their responsibilities may seem to be related to the legal field only but they moral attitudes for which they are established can have deeper impact on the social, political, and economics field as well.

The collusion of some state institutions with the economic influencers are well-known. In that arena of increasing personal interests and benefits over public interests, these institutions are supposed to act as ray of hope for all instead of breeding own attitudes and behavior. Today that collusion is joined by a so called civil society, nonprofits and NGOs who serve very narrow agendas.

It is only a matter of time and correction of senses where this decline in standards by the institutions will reach a point of critical proportion leading to closure of them. The rising social movements of Gujarat, Maharashtra and other parts of India shows that citizens have lost their faith in these institutions for protection of their fundamental rights.

It is certainly true that at the outset these movements seem to be more political in nature rather than social or economical. But these narratives are also created by the actors of media and academic elites with inflexions towards polity and personal benefits rather than society.

*To say that public trust is eroded in critical institutions is an understatement. The rising crimes with little or no solution in foresight tell us how grim the situation will be in future.*

*And in that, having institutions who likes to be judged on the limited incidents of successes is a trapped mentality. They will project those limited successes as some kind of antidote to all their failures. The cases are taken to get praise from a legion instead of continuous effort towards a moral attitude where Dharma will praise them. But it is not just the fault of these institutions.*

*The stalling of these institutions is promoted by a legion of activists, media and ideologies. The legion, about whom Oscar*

Wilde observed while writing his quote. For them whether it is equality or it is human rights, both exist for people in coherence to ideology. Sometimes it seems that reviews by United Nations are genuine and a warning for us to correct those institutions and make them more autonomous. But when they use their power arbitrarily it becomes a matter of concern on accountability and dedication towards the moral attitude for which they are established.

I hope that one day Dharma will make everything clear to them, so that the idea of Oscar Wilde becomes subjective rather than having people or institutions with subjective morality. People who don't hide behind false provisions or lie and work with the principle of

कर्मण्येवाधिकारस्ते मा फलेषु कदाचन।

मा कर्मफलहेतुर्भूर्मा ते सङ्गोऽस्त्वकर्मणि॥

(Karmanye vadhikaraste Ma Phaleshu Kadachana,

Ma Karma Phala Hetur Hurma Te Sangostvakarmani)

Meaning: let's not the fruits of action be your motive, nor let your attachment be to inaction.

ॐ 3

## The Two Hearings I attended in the Supreme Court

When **I** **T**ried to **C**ontrovert **T**hese **I**deologies

*Every day we do a lot of communication. Whether we are at home, office, school or any public place we communicate. We communicate our ideas, our wishes or just communicate on things happening around us. If we add non-verbal means of communication like facial expressions, gestures, paralanguage, haptics etc. it becomes a web of intentions and messages for others.*

*For people at high authorities conveying such ideas or messages on large scale becomes far easier because of the access to wider reach official platforms and invitations to speak at gatherings. But at the same time it makes it difficult for them to hide their ideologies as their actions are always under close scrutiny. The moment they bypass those ideas someone at somewhere will observe them and if that person knows Dharma, he/she will try to controvert those authorities in order to protect the dharma.*

## Introduction

Our discussion on Natural Justice (Chapter 1) had one key thing in it which was left for later discussion. That thing was the second major idea of the principle of Natural Justice as **Audi Alteram Partem,** a Latin phrase meaning "*Let the other side be heard as well*" or the right to fair hearing.

The principle of audi alteram partem provides an opportunity to be heard or a safety from condemnation without being heard. Hearing, which extends a fair opportunity to raise questions or give answers. While in legal terms a mere fact that a decision affects rights or interests is sufficient to subject the decision to the procedures required by natural justice but we have seen that how some people at will call those interests as official or representative capacity and create inroads to the cause of Justice.

The four judges of the Supreme Court in their press conference displayed that judges aren't just the adjudicators but they act as a counsel for one side also. Today, these ideologies run so deep that we have judgments based on own knowledge rather than the enlightened knowledge gained in the case leading to different judgments by judges hearing the case at same and different time.

## The Hurdles in accepting my petition

As I told earlier, in October I filed the petition and in December I removed the defects, leaving the courts with little options but to put in front of the judges. But the little options were my viewpoint. A petition for protection of fundamental rights with no defects is not the sure shot way to get heard by judges.

So, from January to March I kept getting the replies that my petition will be forwarded in few days. Finally, in March I felt that enough is enough; I should personally visit the Court for the progress on the matter. But that would have yielded nothing if I had not approached the Public Relations Officer (PRO) at Supreme Court.

Initially, the PRO too seemed to be busy with some people on private case, as it took nearly two hours of wait before he finished that decision and called me. After 2 hours of wait the PRO meet me and called one person to do the follow up. After the follow up from that person the PIL-Writ section found that my file is lying in the office of Lodging Registrar because of which the PIL-WRIT Section kept telling that it may be with WRIT Section and WRIT Section was telling that it will be with PIL-WRIT Section.

## The falsehood from Lodging Registrar

Locating file is one thing and processing it is another. In our procedural setup we have two kinds of rules or procedures, as:

1. The first kind of Rules are the rules which can help the authorities to overlook some conditions if the petition helps in propagation of their ideology or get publicity.

2. The second kind of rules are the rules which give them power to not consider petitions which are against their decisions, dear beliefs etc. even if all other conditions are met.

My petition was of second kind. So, the second kind of rules which were applied by them and this time it was the Lodging Registrar who tried to do that.

As I told earlier that finally on my visit the Supreme Court administrative staff was able to locate my file and told that soon the status will updated. So, the first update by them on my petition was to show defects in my petition. This time (after curing all the old defects) the number of defects was 140.

The messages which we can think from it were two:

1. In my earlier petition I had 20 defects and now in the process of removing those defects I made 140 fresh defects, or

2. The administrative section wants to show that how deep the support for ideologies which I have challenged is.

The first message of large number of defects was created by repeating 20 defects 7 times to give an inflated figure 140 defects. It may be an attempt to discourage my efforts. I reported the same with my outrage on it to PRO. Next day the errors were removed from the online page and the status of petition changed to old under consideration. Around 10 days later, I received a letter from Registrar telling me that my petition is cancelled because of certain reasons as follows:

-2-

The perusal of the records shows that apparently the petitioner intends to assail the findings recorded by this Hon'ble Court in Writ Petition(C) No. 274 of 2014(Ram Singh & Ors. Vs. Union of India) whereby the benefit of reservation extended to the Jats had been held to be bad in the eyes of law and the notification dated 4.03.2014 had come to be quashed by a judgment and order dated 17.3.2015. So is the question of law propounded by the petitioner in the petition. Over and apart the petitioner has made incoherent and vague submissions, which are difficult to comprehend and decipher.

Infact, innumerable Interlocutory Applications for clarifications, directions and modifications have come to be filed in W.P.(C) No. 274 of 2014 from time to time. All the interim application already stand disposed off.

The petitioner had also filed a Review Petition(C) No. 3539 of 2016 in I.A. No. 19 in I.A. D. No. 2545 of 2016 which has also been dismissed by this Hon'ble Court on 21.02.2017.

The narrations hereinabove categorically go to show that petitioner intends to assail the findings recorded by this Hon'ble Court in Writ Petition(C) No. 274 of 2014. I am afraid the judicial proceedings of this Hon'ble Court and that too after having attained finality cannot be now allowed to be assailed under Article 32 of the Constitution of India. The said proposition of law is by now fairly well settled. Reference may aptly be made in this behalf to the ratio laid down in judgments in A.R. Antulay Vs. R.S. Nayak & Anr. (1988) 2 SCC 602), this Hon'ble Court relying upon a decision of the nine Judge Bench of this Hon'ble Court in Naresh Shridhar Marajikar & Ors. Vs. State of Maharashtra & Anr. (1966 (3) SCR 744) concluded that the judicial proceedings of this Hon'ble Court are not subject to the writ jurisdiction under Article 32 of the Constitution. So is the view taken

-3-

by this Hon'ble Court in Ajit Kumar Barat Vs. Secretary, Indian Tea Association & Ors. (2001) 5 SCC 42).

For all the reasons discussed hereinabove, I am of the considered view that the present petition does not disclose any reasonable cause to be entertained for registration under the provisions of Order XV, Rule 5 of the Supreme Court Rules, 2013. It is ordered accordingly.

Petitioner-in-person be informed.

But consider the reliefs sought by me against which the Ld. Registrar had following observations:

Constitution of India seeking the following reliefs:-

i)    Identification and transfer of right to possession of RAMJANAMBHOOM to Aryans.

ii)    The government should be directed to either include an Aryan in any of the Vedic teaching served by it or make a disclaimer while teaching that actual interpretation of Veda may differ because of no prior consideration and approval by Aryans.

iii)    Provide Aryans the option of choosing their Ayans religion while filling government forms.

iv)    On reconsideration of WRIT PETITION(CIVIL) NO.274 OF 2014 judgment, I leave it you whether you are satisfied with the arguments made in the petition or not, whether justice should be based on facts or ideology, whether procedure has the power to suppress truth.

v)    Else, pardon me for any offensive word(if used earlier), but free myself from your jurisdiction. Being from the same community as to which Shri Ram belonged and having a life based on Shri Ram dharma, I feel strangulated to have a kangaroo court jurisdiction over me which can blatantly pass judgments based on the ideological and community impulses. I know what my dharma is and I don't need the authority of an institution which is highly biased and opinionated in its decisions

The Petition has been filed through e-filing.

The first three reliefs categorically speak about my Fundamental Rights as an Aryan and Guaranteed by the Constitution of India under Article 21, 25 and 29. But the Ld. Registrar picked the fourth relief which I left to the judges on being satisfied with my arguments.

Even if avoid the argument of reliefs sought. Consider the points given by him for cancellation:

1. The first point is that submissions are vague and incoherent with intention to assail the judgment. This is the prime tool of the forces of Adharma i.e. to defame others. It is strange that during the defects no Assistant Registrar pointed that. Also, if the submissions are vague and incoherent, then Courts are duty bound to provide legal help not to cancel them. The language used by me contained no such word which isn't used by the Judges in court. It seems that the Ld. Registrar was unaware of the Supreme Court Judgments language.

2. The second important tool of the forces of Adharma is Falsehood. The Ld. Registrar wrote that the petitioner filed one review petition 3539 of 2016 in IA no. 19 in IA D. no. 2545/2016. But every person is free to search about that. I have categorically stated and signed in my petition that on this matter I have not filed any petition in this court or any other court.

In fact, in my life I have filed only one petition and that was the petition which was under consideration. Only ld. Registrar can tell that on what basis or how he found that I filed that petition. For reference I have attached an image of that also which clearly states that whose case it was. I'm not an advocate who will go and file cases for others. It was filled by someone else. But in his duty to reject the petition Ld. Registrar attached it to me. I told that to his staff also in my communication but he never accepted his fault.

S U P R E M E   C O U R T   O F   I N D I A
RECORD OF PROCEEDINGS

R.P.(C) NO. 3539/2016
IN
I.A.NO. 19
IN
I.A.D.NO. 2545/2016
IN
W.P.(C) NO. 274/2014

DHYAN PAL SINGH & ANR.                          PETITIONER(S)

VERSUS

BANK OF BARODA                                  RESPONDENT(S)
[WITH APPLN.(S) FOR C/DELAY IN FILING REVIEW PETITION]

Date : 21/02/2017 This petition was circulated today.

CORAM :
        HON'BLE MR. JUSTICE RANJAN GOGOI
        HON'BLE MR. JUSTICE PRAFULLA C. PANT

By Circulation

UPON perusing papers the Court made the following
ORDER

3. The third point given for the rejection of petition was that the case is now settled. The tool of selective ignorance used by forces of Adharma. While finding cases to support his decision he mentioned cases but forget that we have Rupa Ashok Hurra vs Ashok Hurra, 2002 case which came after all those cases and opened a window of opportunity to have a Curative petition. As I needed some changes in the procedure because of violation of the principle of Natural Justice under the present procedure, so I added an appeal for that. But the way of working for forces of Adharma is to first make a decision and then search support for that.

So, I was forced to move an **Appeal by Way of Motion** under **order XV, Rule 5** of the **Supreme Court Rules, 2013** to challenge the contentions of Lodging Registrar. The submission of Appeal by Way of Motion from my side was the stage from where the violations of the principle of **"Audi Alteram Partem"** started.

The principle of audi alteram partem, in words of Supreme Court of India means that no man should be condemned unheard or that both the sides must be heard before passing any order. A man cannot incur the loss of property or liberty for an offence by a judicial proceeding until he has a fair opportunity of answering the case against him.

In words of De Smith, during Judicial Review of Administrative Action (1980), at page 161, "Where a statute authorizes interference with properties or other rights and is silent on the question of hearing, the courts would apply rule of universal application and founded on plainest principles of natural justice."

Similarly, Wade in Administrative Law (1977) at page 395 says "principles of natural justice operate as implied mandatory requirements, non-observance of which invalidates the exercise of power." Supreme Court of India till A.K. Kraipak's case (supra) believed that the rules of natural justice are to supplement the law of the land and operate only in areas not covered by any law validly made.

But in the case of Smt. Maneka Gandhi v. Union of India and another, AIR 1978 SC 597, Supreme Court of India also changed its observations and observed that even where there is no specific provision for showing cause, yet in a proposed action which affects the rights of an individual it is the duty of the authority to give reasonable opportunity to be heard. This duty is said to be implied by nature of function to be performed by the authority having power to take punitive or damaging action.

## My first Hearing in the Court of Justice Sanjay Kishan Kaul

The filling of Appeal by Way of Motion from my side became a tense situation for the concerned Registrar as his power of rejecting a petition was challenged. So, they again tried to play the game of defects but this time I read the Supreme Court Rules, 2013 thoroughly and told them in clear cut manner that I'm not going to do anything further.

It is your wish to accept the things as they are or list the matter in Chamber of Judges for directions whether today or after 90 days of defect removal time. The Supreme Court Rules, 2013 provides that "If defects are not removed in 90 days, the matter shall be listed with office report on default before the Hon'ble Chamber Judge for appropriate orders."

Soon the 90 day window passed and the day came when I got my first opportunity to controvert the ideologies and I did that without any fail. The conversation was like this:

**Me**: Good Morning Sir.

**Justice Kaul**: Hmm and started looking the file.

**Me**: Sir, with your permission may I use Hindi.

**Justice Kaul**: Ok.

**Me**: Supreme Court of India in its Judgment on cancellation of Jat Reservation was convinced with the arguments of NCBC that Jat is the best representative of Vedic Aryan. As, Jat is Aryan and in words of Sage Valmiki Lord Ram was the best Vedic Aryan of his time. So, by that analogy Jat is the best person to have claim on the Ram Janmabhoomi.

**Justice Kaul**: But it is yet to be decided whether Ram existed or not.

**Me**: Sir, till Allahabad High Court we don't have any doubt on his existence. Regarding the order of Ld. Registrar, I have not filed any other petition in my life but the Registrar has pointed that my earlier petition was rejected. My challenge on the Jat Reservation is for the Curative petition which is permissible under Rupa Ashok Hurra vs Ashok Hurra, 2002. But the registrar has played that portion as the main argument of my petition. When I made that clear in my appeal by way of motion they are saying that my format is not well. I have checked the Supreme Court Rules, its website and other major online portals on legal procedures etc. but none has the so called format of the petition.

**Justice Kaul**: Please file your appeal with defects being cured or tell them about the non-availability of format. I'm giving you time of 4 weeks.

**Me**: Please extend it to 8 weeks and the judge extended the same.

**Justice Kaul**: Ok. Submit it in 8 weeks.

So, within the time limits I filled the Appeal by Way of Motion with added mentions on the directions given by the Hon'ble Judge. Though the judge had little to speak about the illogical or the irrational conclusions drawn by the lodging registrar but I was yet to realize that for judges it is the office report which matters more than the actual situation or the reasoning given by the petitioner.

## My second Hearing in the Court of CJI and two other Judges

Finally, after a big wait of 4 months with fulfillment of few more formalities time came when I was allowed to appear and argue in the court of Chief Justice of India. The conversation was like this:

**Me**: Good Morning Sir's.

**CJI and others**: Busy looking down the file.

**Me**: Sir, with your kind permission may I use Hindi as and when required.

**CJI**: Yes, use it with full openness.

**Me**: In Writ Petition Civil 274 of 2014, Supreme Court of India while cancelling the Jat Reservation observed that, "If the view taken by NCBC is an impossible and perverse view, the government can go against the advice given by NCBC. So, first I will show how the view taken by NCBC was an impossible and perverse view.

All three judges started to look my file carefully. One Judge pointed the attention of the CJI to something in the file and all laughed. After a pause of few seconds:

**CJI**: Who are you?

**Me**: Subhash Chandra Gahlawat.

**CJI**: Repeated the same question in Hindi, "Nahi Tum ho Kaun" (No, who are you)?

**Me**: I'm a Jat.

**CJI**: What brings you here?

**Me**: I filed a writ petition on the violation of my fundamental rights and for the same I'm here.

**CJI**: After a pause. You have used abusive language against the court. Your petition is dismissed.

(The judges who give lectures on freedom of expression and fairness in Justice system during public speeches. The Judges who project themselves as the protectors of Human Rights and what not just rejected the petition without any hearing on the petition).

**Me**: At least you will hear what I want to say.

**The person standing behind me** (Probably the advocate waiting for next matter) in low voice: Brother, it is Supreme Court.

**Me**: Then What? Does it mean that they will not hear people?

**Reactions of CJI and other Judges during this**: While CJI kept looking down, other Judges lifted the head looked at me at one or two times and then started looking down.

I waited for around half a minute. But the judges rarely looked upward and kept themselves busy by looking downwards.

Finally, the security guard standing near me said that Ok Brother! They don't want to listen and I moved out of the court.

But the most flagrant thing was that after hearing nothing the judges in their order said that we heard the applicant in-person and dismissed it.

It seems that the Judge wanted to ignite the passion. He repeated the same question with the hope that the person will speak something abusive. When I said nothing what he wanted to hear, he speculated things and spoke what he wanted to have as a reason for not hearing the petition.

Even, I'm yet to believe myself that despite such blatant lies and disgrace to dharma I remained calm and not said much. It looks absurd when the same judges at National Law Day or at various functions project themselves as the saviors of our democracy, rights of people and most importantly Dharma but in real they are nothing but the people who in the guise of Dharma works for Adharma.

## The way to keep procedural fairness

The fundamental principle of fair procedure requires a fair opportunity of hearing. An opportunity with the freedom to raise questions or answer the false views considered as truth against them. In UK, from where we have the origins of our modern-day systems, this error was rectified as early as in 1963 (Ridge v Baldwin), where Lord Reid reviewed the authorities extensively and attacked the problem at its root by demonstrating how the term judicial had been misinterpreted as requiring some additional characteristic over and above the characteristic that the power affected some person's rights.

In words of Lord Reid: the mere fact that the power affects rights or interests is what makes it "judicial" and so subjects the whole exercise to the procedures required by natural justice. While judiciary has used this interpretation of procedural fairness as a means to intervene in cases of judicial review but when it comes to the procedural fairness in own works they neglect those considerations.

Fair hearing is incomplete without an opportunity to be heard. Every person has the right to have a hearing and be allowed to present his or her own case. And where the petitioner is the aggrieved person oral hearing becomes important. As Lord Phillips observed, *"if the wider public are to have confidence in the justice system, they need to be able to see that justice is done rather than being asked to take it on trust"*.

When we vest certain powers in a person, we expect a fair character from him while exercising that authority. The decisions of Dharma are based on unbiased hearing. During the war of Ramayana, Lord Ram tried his best to convince Ravana about Dharma and display the Adharma in his actions and the impacts of that.

But Ravana made that Adharma as the goal of his life. And to protect that goal he was forced to commit more and more actions in violation of Dharma. Similarly, when modern-day decision makers make a judgment which is in violation of Dharma it becomes important on their part to change that decision at the very first instance of getting attention to it.

If instead of Dharma they make that decision as their life goal, they are bound to follow the path of Adharma and take actions based on the tools of Adharma. The one poor decision has made the whole institution to spread lies, ill will and hatred against others. The decision has forced them to reject petitions even before hearing it. But they forgot that in their acts they are violating even the principles of Natural Justice, like audi alteram partem.

A judge should always remember that his/her duty is of:
**"Krinvanto Vishwam Aryam- Make this World a noble place to live in"**
By moving it from
**"Asato ma sadgamaya- From unrighteousness to righteousness"**
**"Tamaso ma jyotirgamaya- From darkness to light"**
**Mrityorma amritam gamaya- From mortality towards immortality"**

ॐ 4

## Reservation

**T**he **R**oot of **A**ll **I**lls

A child is born with 50% genetic (biological) similarity with each parent. That similarity goes deep in his biological makeup, leading to 25% genetic similarity with grandparents, 12.5% with great grandparents and so on till 7 generation. In those 7 generations he/she is connected to many people and in a set up like India it becomes natural to identify with a certain subspecies or Jati, a sub-component of Species or Parjati.

But that scientific knowledge was replaced by some social considerations and ignorant people formed a thing like reservation from that. Reservation is a tool to create a special class of people to have easier access to education and economic resources (which also depends on the education). Add to that the exercise was so nonsense that people who had 700 years of rule were given reservation while the people who resisted those 700 years and preserved their culture under the rule of a book guided person were ignored. Therefore, it becomes natural that people who are not given those benefits will demand the same benefits to have equality of opportunities.

## Introduction

Reservation is among the most absurd things in the history of Independent India. If reservation was an absurd thing from start, our politicians and institutions added many more absurdities to it leading to the increased demands for reservation by others as well.

Before the start of British rule in parts of India (1750's) the population of India was only 12-13crore. By 1872, when the first official census of modern time happened, it was nearly 24crore. Please remember that during that time many parts of Indian subcontinent like Pakistan, Bangladesh etc were part of India.

Today, with 1.21 billion people we have a population density of 382 person/sq km. So, we can say that by any means the population density was around 75-80 person per sq km or less in 1872. In 1750's it was only around 40 people per sq km. If we go more back in history it might have been very low.

This means that a lot of area of India was without any possession. The same is visible in our history where despite being a plain area with no geographical barriers many parts of Great Indian plain were open spaces with no human settlement. Under such conditions many people because of small size, lack of unity or absence of zeal to establish own settlements choose to live at the outskirts of prevalent societies.

Suppose, in today's so called Rule of Law time, if an unknown person comes to your house will you give him space in your home? So, the people settled at the outside. Everyone knows that in old times what kind of infrastructure was prevalent in India. Famines and water scarcity were common. So, it was natural that people kept control over own resources. Even today we lack that basic infrastructure in many villages.

Under such conditions British came to India with little or no knowledge of India and Dharma, but intent and determination to rule India. So they placed too much of false propaganda in the Indian Society. One such was the historical oppression of some people.

E.g. the so called Father of Evolution and a British Citizen Charles Darwin with his half-cousin Galton tried to replicate the Indian ways but In India They called identification with the people connected to you through blood as socially derogatory practice. They gave it the name of caste groups and projected that as sources of oppression. This worked in their favor.

Based on that experience, they kept dividing people and people believed in their education and value system. Those ideas were carried on by Indians even after independence and reservation was introduced. Later, that reservation was increased and even those people who had a continuous rule of 700 years and used to distribute titles to others on service were included in the new list.

The new list also had many people who were just like the others who were not made part of it, in terms of social and economic conditions. Today when a normal child looks around himself and found people who were less hard-working and meritorious than himself are given an easy path to achieve the dreams and aspirations which are becoming so important in the present conditions of society, it is natural that he/she will rebel.

Add to that, the recent Oxfam study says that top 1% of Indian population corners 73% of wealth generated in India. The Finance minister of India said in the parliament that only 24.4lakh people have reported income above 10lakh and 76lakh with above 5lakh income. It comes out to be less than 0.1 % and nearly 0.7% of India.

Even if we double the numbers because of black money or non-reporting we will have very few Indians with income above 5lakh. In that situation we have a OBC reservation with identification of creamy layer (i.e. no reservation benefit) to income above 6lakh (now increased to 8lakh). Plus we have a Commission for OBC, according to which even if the income of a person who is part of the list earns above 20lakh from first source of income, his son or daughter will enjoy reservation benefit. So, what on earth makes the rest of 30-35% population resource rich that those people don't need reservation?

Therefore, we have Jat, Patel, Maratha and many other communities either demanding reservation or wanting change in the kind of reservation given to them. This demand for the same benefits by other communities who are yet to have those benefits has created a sense of threat among the people who are enjoying it.

So, they attempt to create inroads in the demands of other communities with the hope that they can influence the people with little knowledge or lack of awareness on dharma will be influenced by it. The misfortune of our time is that we have many people who in want of showing their half-baked knowledge easily accept those ideas of Adharma and believe themselves as protectors of this Adharma.

## The absurdity of Reservation

For proper understanding of the absurdities behind the reservation what we need is to have an objective mindset with ability to analyze the things in the past as well as how the things of present will shape in future.

The story of reservation starts from the early knowledge system of India known as Vedas. In India, for long Vedas are considered as the main source of knowledge. Vedas focused a lot on the people and society what we will learn in the part 2 of the book and serves as the essence of Dharma.

For our learning on reservation we need to know that Vedas being concerned with the study of laws of nature and have a life according to the laws of nature, identified people to have differences at genetic, mental and other levels. For social categorization of people they used Gunas and for the biological categorization of the people they used Jati, a subspecies division of the Human species or Parjati.

But some people from outside of India manipulated that knowledge for own benefits. E.g. the ideas of Jati, no marriage among close relatives and so on are nothing but the natural outcomes of the so called "Theory of Evolution" given by Charles Darwin. Even he tried to have a system like the Vedic system in England by discouraging the cousin-marriages etc.

Coming to the Vedas, being a practical form of knowledge the teachings of Vedas were made part of the social and culture complex of Vedic people. And in that set up the formal education of Vedas was largely restricted to the people who can help in progression of that knowledge and few high position authorities who are responsible for the implementation of that knowledge.

While Vedas are the deepest source of knowledge till date, that doesn't mean that the whole India was following it. Parts of South India has own education system. North East had its own. In between some had Buddhism, Jainism and so on to guide the education and lifestyle system. Before the coming of British Power in India we had Mughals who dominated the large parts of India and we are yet to show anything from that time which can show that they worked for the education of people.

So, no one can claim that education was a privilege of the some castes only. Still on our independence certain false narratives were placed by the policy makers and many people were made to believe that because of the large support by the British intellectuals to that idea. Let's look at the real and imaginary situations field-wise:

## Economy:

- If we consider the economic system than large part of India was largely rural. In 1901, only 10.84% population was Urban, while 89.16% as Rural. By 1951 the urban population was increased to 17.3% and the rural population was 82.7%.

- So, no one can claim that having access to urban infrastructure or land in cities was the privilege of specific communities.

- The Economic progress of India during the British rule was a Zero-sum game with 1% annual increase from 1880 to 1920. Agriculture remained the main contributor to the economy as well the main employer for the population because of the high rural population.

- The modern jobs and economic system like railways, banks, transport, hotels, power generation etc. were just starting to emerge. So, no one can say that the certain communities had an advantage in certain things.

## Education:

- In terms of Education the Literacy Rate of India in 1901 was:

| Province | Male Literacy % | Female Literacy % |
|---|---|---|
| Madras | 11.9 | 0.9 |
| Bombay | 11.6 | 0.9 |
| Bengal | 10.4 | 0.5 |
| Assam | 8.5 | 0.3 |
| Punjab | 6.7 | 0.4 |
| United Provinces | 5.7 | 0.2 |
| Central Provinces | 5.4 | 0.2 |

- By 1951 it increased to 18.33% with 27.16% for Male and 8.86% for Female.

- But this is literacy, not education. Literacy means just the ability to read and write. In 1872, the first census of India only 3.2% Indian had the ability to read and write in any one language. And by 1951 it became 18.33%. Even those literacy figures are of crude literacy rate not effective or complete education. Many of them left education in the school only. So, no one can say that only some communities had access to modern-day knowledge or have literate people while others not.

But the tragedy of our nation is that despite any significant difference of situations people were told that certain communities are socially and economically backward and need reservation in government jobs and educational system. The policymakers and social scientists projected that ancestors of some communities had access to education while others not, so we need to give them reservation in education.

## Health and Sanitation:

Indus Valley Civilization is considered as the first and last city level drainage system of India before the arrival of British. After that we had little evidence to say that cities had some kind of drainage system. Only some forts can claim to have a drainage system. From that time to till today we have little toilet facilities in villages or even the cities that we needed to have people for cleaning.

When in 2014-2015 we have to set targets of fulfilling the needs of sanitation by developing 111 million toilets in 5 years, one can identify the shortage of toilets. But at the time of independence the people were told that for centuries their ancestors employed people of certain communities for the cleaning of those toilets, thus requiring a reservation for them.

The truth is that the employers of these kind of jobs i.e. railways and municipalities were the creation of the British Rule. British people had issues with open defecation so they started to employ people for cleaning. Later some Indians also adopted that lifestyle leading to people being employed for that.

## Land Holdings:

For long, people are told that while your ancestors had access to good land but others had little or no land holdings. So, certain people needed reservation because of no land assets. When I look at the history of India particularly the region of Haryana, it was the Bharata Tribe with others who won the battle against King Sudas leading to establishment of Jat control over the land in Haryana, Western Uttar Pradesh and other regions. Later, the Ikshvakus, Kurus, Pandavas etc. spread it to other parts.

After the end of that we had nominal commands of Mauryans, Harsha and other till Mughals over the land of Haryana with Jat remaining the main land holders. But that doesn't mean that the whole land of the region was under Jat dominance. People lived in villages which were spread here and there. E.g. till 12th century Jhajjar district is considered to have only one village as inhabited village while all other land was free land.

In that system certain people came from other parts of India and instead of clearing and living on the open lands they accepted to live on the outskirts of the established villages to have food grains for the skills offered by them.

Today it is projected as the oppression from our ancestors where they lived at the centre of village and had control over land. But the other communities were stopped from land possession and have a dwelling place in the centre. It is just like modern-day situation where migrants from various parts or from neighboring countries come in search of work and starts living on the outskirts of cities.

Few decades or centuries later they become a part of the prevalent living system in the region and then project themselves as long being oppressed by the main communities. E.g. In Haryana the same feelings were expressed by people who came to Haryana as refugee during the partition and now claim themselves as the oppressed community.

But at the time of independence our ancestors were fooled that these communities are oppressed by your ancestors for long. While you had land with assets, they had none. Thus they need special considerations and reservation in jobs so that they can get jobs and education.

With these false narratives the idea of reservation was pushed and in a period of 3-4 decades almost 65% of Indian population was given reservation benefits.

**The demands for reservation by Jat, Maratha, Patel, Kapu and others**

If we look at the situations which prevailed from independence to 1980 and even till 1990's we had a living style where the society rather than the government had the main hold over the people. E.g. when India got its independence the laws which were made had given due space to the community laws and rules in that.

So, the people had no issue with the reservation of others. But today the situations have changed. Whether it is the legislative, executive or Judiciary all want to extend their power and hold over the society. Some are so obsessed with power that even with little knowledge they will project themselves as superior. E.g. recently in Supreme Court of India we had a case where the idea of Sapinda-based marriage was challenged.

Any person with knowledge of India and its history knows that these ideas are related to the Maharishi Bharadwaja and Kashyapa where a person is discouraged to marry in 7 generations and the scientific rationale for that was very well observed by the Charles Darwin and Gregor Mendel (the father of Evolution and Father of Genetics).

At the time of Independence the lawmakers accepted that and give due space in the laws. But some judges with scant knowledge about India said that these ideas are **Louis XV** ways of rule and we have no place for that. Whether it was the time of Maharishi Bharadwaja (nearly 7000 BC) or the present day the child still have 50% genetic similarity with mother and 50% with Father.

When we extend the same to 7 generations we reach a situation where the individual genetic similarity with the potential mate becomes less than 1% and the probability of having a genetic disease to the child out of the nearly 6000 known genetic diseases is reduced by a significant amount. The details of it are very well documented by Maharishi Gautama and others.

It is law of nature and as Lord Ram said:

**"The will of God is expressed through the laws of nature"**

The people who understood laws of nature try to have life by that. But people with no or little knowledge of Dharma and nature will try to manipulate our thoughts and impose their irrational and unscientific ideas over others with hope of gaining power in society.

Like this, in recent past various government bodies and their interference in the life of people has increased so much that people want to become a part of that. Government jobs and posts are becoming the dreams and aspirations of people. This can also be gauged from the increased interests of students from premium colleges of India in the government jobs.

This increased interest is also the reason because of which the old bluffs of reservation are coming out and many people are becoming conscious of the pathetic reservation policy and arguments used for extension of this reservation. E.g. as per NSSO Survey, 46% of Indian Landholdings with 52% of Big Farmers holding are with OBC communities. The identification of creamy layer has a special mention of considering agriculture holding not income for identification of creamy layer.

Still the first argument which is given to neglect the demands of Jat, Maratha, Kapus or others is that the OBC reservation is not for people with agricultural landholdings. If OBC reservation isn't for farming communities then why so many agricultural landholdings are with OBC communities and why NCBC has agriculture criteria for identification of creamy layer?

In that debate some social scientists or policymakers with little or no knowledge of society will join and project that because of decreased income from agriculture people had started to look for government jobs and demand reservation. If we look at the history we will find that where was the money at the first place that one can say that the decreased income is the reason for demands for reservation.

Everyone knows about how inadequate the market for agriculture products was and for large part of Human history the products of agriculture are used for self-consumption and for direct exchange of goods and services.

It is not the money but the value of a thing that matters. Unfortunately, in recent times it is this decrease in the value of agriculture and the increase in the value of a government job in society that people want to be a government servant. E.g. as we depicted above a situation where people with scant knowledge become a lawmaker and will show their will or ideology as the only truth with scant regard for will of god i.e. laws of nature.

It is natural that people from all communities to get attracted by similar kind of jobs. When people from these communities see that people with same or more means are getting entry in the government jobs with less hard work it is natural to demand the same considerations.

E.g. in 2016, UPSC stopped the joining of 120 OBC candidates out of nearly 300. The main reason was the issue of creamy layer where many students had parents with income above 6 lakh but they availed reservation. This shows the kind of people who are taking benefit of the reservation.

When Jat, Maratha or other communities see that, it is natural for them to demand the same considerations. This is where the forces of Adharma enters the scene and starts the vicious propaganda against their demands. All of them clubbed together to project a myth or falsehood as the only truth. We have discussed some actors earlier and now we will extend our coverage to the two main actors in the next two chapters, as:

1. National Commission for Backward Classes (NCBC) and

2. Media including the print and electronic media.

*Every falsehood has a shelf-life. The joining of different actors may increase that shelf-life in that moment but at the end of the day it is only the dharma which should prevail. The absurdities in reservation are long and to protect those absurdities Supreme Court reposed the power to decide the inclusion, exclusion etc. in NCBC.*

*The same NCBC which during the demands of other communities will show an income of 2-3lakh rupee as income enough to avoid reservation benefits but for own communities will say that the income criterion of 6lakh rupee is wrongly applied. As per NCBC the income criteria of 6lakh for existing OBC people is not for the salary and agriculture income but for other income or the second income. The first income can be anything.*

*For them the reservation to other communities become a political doll but they give warnings of political backlash to parties in power even if the reservation of creamy layer is taken away.*

*Media, who claim it to be neutral and self-proclaimed repository of humanity and knowledge will join them in those absurdities and propagate those false ideologies as the truth. Therefore, what we need to have is an objective mindset and awareness on the precedents and present realities to call the bluff of the forces of Adharma and protect the Dharma.*

ॐ 5

**Objective Analysis of the Supreme Court judgment and NCBC report**

**A**ctual **B**ias: The **F**oundations of the **S**upreme **C**ourt of **I**ndia **J**udgment

The basic difference between the dharma and Adharma is that while dharma has universal considerations with universal goals, Adharma has false considerations with false goals. This difference in the nature of considerations and goals make it mandatory for forces of Adharma to remain as discreet and biased in the approach as they can.

This bias in legal terms can be an actual bias or an apparent bias. Therefore, to save that bias or falsehood, the forces of Adharma will add more and more falsehood to it. But after certain period that falsehood becomes visible to everyone and every sane mind should identify that and question the forces of Adharma instead of serving the cause of Adharma by increasing the strength of the forces of Adharma.

## Introduction

If we read the Supreme Court Judgment against Jat Reservation, we will find that the judgment was largely based on the NCBC report on Jat Reservation where it recommended to government that NCBC report is to be followed by government until and unless the view taken by NCBC is an impossible and false view.

The same view which I wanted to project in the Supreme Court on the hearing of my Petition. Any person who has done a reading on the NCBC report can tell on the very first reading that it was a biased report. But still it was accepted and projected as a report with full of justifications.

Therefore, in order to protect the Dharma it becomes important that the false foundations or cover used by the forces of Adharma should be exposed to the people. In this chapter, we will discuss that report and will show how biased the whole report is, which the forces of Adharma feels as a gospel truth.

## The Judgment from Supreme Court

Before I start my analysis and arguments on the NCBC report we should look at some of the observations from Supreme Court Judgment, so that we can identify how much pain it took to have a thorough analysis of the report before coming to the conclusion and cancelling the Jat Reservation.

The conclusions of the Supreme Court start from Para 46 (Page 52 of the Judgment), under heading Our Conclusions. The very first line of the conclusions stress on the point that the NCBC has done a thorough study of the available material (which I will show how much thorough it was) and the second line stress that the decision of not recommending Jat is based on material evidences, reasons and without any extraneous or irrelevant considerations.

These lines of conclusions from Supreme Court judgment are important to know as these lines will show the actual and apparent bias from the judges while considering the NCBC report in detail, a study which should have been done by the Courts.

(*To avoid any distortions in the interpretations or adding any subjective bias in the minds of readers, I have used the images from the Supreme Court Judgment and NCBC report so that the readers should gauge everything on its own, not just to go with my words).*

*Supreme Court Conclusions from Page 52:*

**46.** Undoubtedly, the report dated 26.02.2014 of the NCBC was made on a detailed consideration of the various reports of the State Backward Classes Commissions; other available literature on the subject and also upon consideration of the findings of the Expert Committee constituted by the ICSSR to examine the matter. The decision not to recommend the Jats for inclusion in the Central List of OBCs of the States in question cannot be said to be based on no materials or unsupported by reasons or characterized as decisions arrived at on consideration of matters that are, in any way, extraneous and irrelevant. Having requested the ICSSR to go into the matter and upon receipt of the report of the Expert Committee constituted in this regard, the NCBC was under a duty and obligation to consider the same and arrive at its own

*The next image is of Page 53 showing how Supreme Court Judges tried to undermine the subjective biases or tried to cover up the biases taken in the garb of underplay or overstress by the commission. The time is so limited that despite having the literature available from so long, they remained idle on the decisions for decades and when an ultimatum was given, they said we had very little time.*

either in favour or against the inclusion of the Jats in the Central List of OBCs. The report of the said Body merely recited the facts as found upon the survey undertaken, leaving the eventual conclusion to be drawn by the NCBC. It may be possible that the NCBC upon consideration of the various materials documented before it had underplayed and/or overstressed parts of the said material. That is bound to happen in any process of consideration by any Body or Authority of voluminous information that may have been laid before it for the purpose of taking of a decision. Such an approach, by itself, would not make either the decision making process or the decision taken legally infirm or unsustainable. Something more would be required in order to bypass the advice tendered by the NCBC which judicially (**Indra**

*The next image (Page 54) is an image from the Supreme Court Judgment where it accepted that an impossible and perverse view from NCBC would justify exclusion. I would have proved it long-ago if I had the privilege of having a sane and rational mind in the court who listens to Dharma.*

54

Sawhney) and statutorily (**NCBC Act**) would be binding on the Union Government in the ordinary course. An impossible or perverse view would justify exclusion of the advice tendered but that had, by no means, happened in the present case. The mere possibility of a different opinion or view would not detract from the binding nature of the advice tendered by the NCBC.

## About NCBC, its Report and Analysis of the report:

### 1. Composition

## NATIONAL COMMISSION FOR BACKWARD CLASSES

Hon'ble Shri Justice V. Eswaraiah, Chairperson

Hon'ble Shri S. K. Kharventhan, Member

Hon'ble Shri A. K. Saini, Member

Hon'ble Shri A. K. Mangotra, Member Secretary

### 2. The Basis of the Study of NCBC report

As per NCBC report, its report was made on the basis of the available reports on Jat Reservation, representations made in favor or against the Jat reservation and the available literature including the books which are given a specific reference by the NCBC as books against the Jat Reservation by other OBC. The detailed list of books, reports and number of representations are given in the images as:

26. The following reports are available on the subject of 'Jat' caste/community as referred by the Group of Ministers:

(1) Social Justice Committee Report, Uttar Pradesh (2001)
(2) Socio-Economic Status of Farming Communities in Northern India, Uttar Pradesh (2003)
(3) Caste, Land and Political Power in UP, Uttar Pradesh
(4) Justice Gurnam Singh Commission Report, Haryana (1990)
(5) Justice K.C.Gupta Report, Haryana (2013)
(6) Justice Gummanmal Lodha Commission Report, NCT of Delhi (1999)
(7) Dr. Lipi Mukhopadhyay Report, Delhi (2005)
(8) State Backward Classes Commission's Reports of State Governments of Rajasthan, Madhya Pradesh, Himachal

**REPORTS**

27. Apart from the aforesaid reports, fiftyone representations "in favour of" 'Jat' caste/community for their inclusion in the Central List of Other Backward Classes and fiftyeight representations "against" the inclusion were received till 31-1-2014. During the course of the public hearing and after the closure of the Public Hearing till. 24-2-2014 large number of representations "in favour" and "against" have also been received.

**REPRESENTATIONS**

**28.** A specific reference is required to be mentioned about three books filed "against" the inclusion of 'Jats':

   (1)   Delhi aur Jat (in Hindi), New Delhi by Rajpal Chikara, 2012

   (2)   Jat Ithihas (3rd Edition in Hindi), New Delhi, Surajmal Smarak Shiksha Sanstha by Deshraj Thakur, 2002

AUTHENTICATED

31

*(A.K. Mangotra)*
Member-Secretary
~~for Backward Classes~~

   (3)   The Jats: Their Role & Contribution to the Socio-Economic Life and Polity of North & North-West India, Volume 1, Originals, 1st January, 2004 by

### BOOKS SUBMITTED AGAINST THE JAT RESERVATION

Though we have much more to support the argument that Jat is the best representative of the Vedic Aryan, but I used the available material from the NCBC report including the People of India Project and IIPA report which showed Jat as the best representative of Vedic Aryan and the same I demanded from the Supreme Court.

Strangely, while Supreme Court has acceptance for all other findings of the NCBC and made them binding on the Government but it is yet to tell the government that NCBC also found that who is the best representative of Vedic Aryan and whose interest government should represent in the case of Ram Janmabhoomi.

The Jat community became very powerful during the medieval period. At present about 1/3rd of Jats are Muslims, one-fifth Sikhs and rest are Hindus.

According to some authorities the Jats are Aryan of the same stock as the Rajputs. Jats are better representative of the ancient Vedic Aryan than any member of the three higher castes of the Hindus. Jats, belong to the same ethnic group as the Rajput and Kshatriya. Their stature is mostly tall, complexion fair, eyes dark, hair on face plentiful, head long, nose narrow and prominent but not very long.

**Above: THE READINGS FROM THE SOCIO-ECONOMIC & POLITICAL CONTRIBUTION OF CASTE & ASSOCIATION IN NORTH INDIA BY BRIJ KISHORE SHARMA BOOK**
**Below: IIPA REPORT WHICH WAS EXAMINED BY THE NCBC AND ITS VIEW FROM THAT**

far as the political position is concerned, as per the report in 45 villages two Ministers, six M.L.As., four ward members, five councilors were found, which means that political representation of Jats is very high but not meager as mistakenly stated in the IIPA report. On examination of the report of IIPA, the Commission was of the view that the 'Jat' as a class cannot be treated as a backward class. Ethnically they are at a higher level; they are of Indo Aryan Descent; their educational level is high; and the social status they command is far higher than the ordinary sudras. In the absence of social and educational backwardness coupled with inadequacy of representation in the services, Article 15(4) and 16(4) do not apply for the purpose of treating Jats as a backward class.

But in this book our focus is mainly on displaying the biases in the approach of NCBC. We will discuss in detail about who is Arya? Who is representative of whom and other things in details in the next book.

### 3. The Subjective interpretations of NCBC

- If a Jat says that he is well treated it is acceptable to NCBC and when Jat says that he is not treated well, it becomes a subjective opinion. The below images on observations of NCBC from Lipi Mukhopadhyaya (IIPA) Report and the observations on Justice Gumanmal Lodha Commission Report (Both from Delhi) tells the difference of opinions or subjective interpretations made by the NCBC.

The IIPA have conducted survey covering five districts. The survey was aimed at ascertaining demographic, social, educational and economic status of the community. As per the report of the IIPA with regard to social treatment, 51.1% of the families of Jats felt that they are treated "well", 19.2% of families of Jats felt that they were treated "normally" and 29.7% of families of Jats felt that they are treated as 'inferior". Thus 70.3% of the families of Jats in the NCT area have felt that they are not subjected to any social discrimination. Overwhelming majority of the families have no grievance in regard to their social status. The fact that some of the Jats felt that they were not treated as equals to Brahmins and Kshatriyas, by no stretch of imagination, can be considered as social discrimination lowering the community to the position of a backward class deserving

**ABOVE: EXTRACT ON IIPA REPORT**
**BELOW: EXTRACT ON GUMANMAL LODHA COMMISSION**

(i) "We cannot agree with the above view since it is based on the subjective opinion of the members of the Jat community themselves as regards the alleged social stigma or social ridicule suffered by them. The fact that the Jats are demanding inclusion of their community in the List of Backward Classes and thus they are

AUTHENTICATED

*(A.K. Mangotra)*

127

totally interested in portraying picture of their backwardness, should have cautioned the two professor to collect objective data for ascertaining the social and educational backwardness instead of acting upon the statements of the members of the community".

- If someone is still doubtful of the NCBC views then consider the comparison of NCBC views on IIPA report on Delhi with 2000 Households study from 46 villages of 5 districts in Delhi as a study based on which it can make conclusions but when it comes the Ajit Singh commission report based on the study of similar sample of 2000 Households from 20 villages of 5 districts in Western UP it becomes a small sample size. Another important thing to note is that the population density of Delhi in 2001 was 9,340 person/km sq while that of UP was only 690 person per sq km. This wide difference of population density with the comparative development differences and small villages compensate the differences even if the IIPA report had all 2000 Jat HH while Ajit Singh had few others. The nullity of IIPA report leaves us with nothing in the reports for study of NCBC which can

## 56. Social economic status of farming community in Northern-India by Shri Ajit Kumar Singh (2003)

This small book is a study of "upwardly mobile intermediate and backward farming communities of Western U.P, namely Yadav, Jat, Gujar, Lodh". An assessment has been made of their relative position and has also been compared with the upper castes and SCs/OBCs. But, the study is based on a very small sample of 2000 rural households selected from 20 villages spread over 5 Districts of Western U.P. This is a major weakness of the study.

**ABOVE: AJIT KUMAR SINGH COMMITTEE STUDY ON 4 COMMUNITIES AND THE SAME SAMPLE SIZE**
**BELOW: IIPA COMMITTEE REPORT**

This was another document listed by the GOM and this was a report prepared by the Indian Institute of Public Administration (IIPA) under the guidance of Prof. Mukhopadhyay. The IIPA formulated a structured questionnaire with topics of relevance to the subject and collected a total sample of 2000 households. The objectives of the study were to prepare a data-base for the Jat community in the light of the guidelines provided by the NCBC and to facilitate the decision making with reference to inclusion of Jat community in the OBC list. A total of 46 villages covered by 5 districts in Delhi was surveyed which was aimed at ascertaining demographic, social, educational and economic status of the community. The assessment of social stigma whether or not suffered by Jats was pointedly kept in view by the IIPA.

2.    The outcome of the survey reveals that 70% of the families of Jats in the NCT felt that they are not subjected to any social discrimination. An overwhelming majority of families had no grievances in regard to their social status. As far as the educational backwardness is concerned the report came to a conclusion that the education level or literacy rate is in favour of the Jat community. While the literacy rate of the general population was 83.7%, it was 85.7% for the Jat community. Studying the political level of activity

AUTHENTICATED

of the community, in 45 villages it found 4 ward members, 5 counsellors, 6 MLAs and 2 Ministers. On examining the report of the IIPA, the NCBC came to the following conclusion:-

"However, examination of the report of IIPA leaves no manner of doubt that Jats as a class cannot be treated as a backward class. Ethnically, they are at a higher level; they are of Indo Aryan Descent; their educational level is high; and social status they command his order higher than ordinary shudras. In the absence of social and educational backwardness coupled with inadequacy of representation in the services, Article 15(4) and 16(4) do not apply for the purpose treating the Jat as backward classes".

No case is made out for any review of the advice of the NCBC

be used as an evidence against the inclusion of Jat Representation except the so called representations against the Jat Reservation.

- Now consider the Representations made against the Jat Reservation from various states/UT's to NCBC in the next figures. The identities of people who came against the inclusion of Jat reservation clearly shows that how much the inclusion of Jat reservation is against the interests of present OBC communities. Though we don't need to prove the imputed bias but the names display abundantly that how much it was an imputed bias for the Judge also.

DELHI

## REPRESENTATIONS AGAINST INCLUSION OF JAT OF DELHI

Sub :-Against Inclusion of "Jat" of Delhi.

By:-

(51) Shri Charan Singh Yadav, Najafgarh, New Delhi- 110043

(52) Acharya Mahavir Singh Shastri, General Secretary, (Akhil Bhartiya Prajapati Kumbhkar Sangh) (Regd.), New Delhi- 110055

(53) Dr. P.C. Patanjali, (Most Backward Classes Federation of India), Shalimar Bag, Delhi- 110088

(54) Dr. P.C. Patanjali, (Akhil Bhartiya Ati Pichra Varg Mahasangh), New Delhi- 110045

(55) Dr. P.C. Patanjali, (Most Backward Classes Federation of India), Shalimar Bag, Delhi- 110088

(56) Shri Ram Sharan Bhati, Executive President, (Akhil Bhartiya Gujar Mahasabha), Padpadganj, New Delhi- 110091

(57) Dr. P.C. Patanjali, (Most Backward Classes Federation of India), Shalimar Bagh, Delhi- 110088

(58) Dr. Pramod Nagar, Advocate, Delhi.

(59) Shri Subodh Kumar, H.No. 345, Munirka, New Delhi- 110002

(60) Shri Ram Sharan Bhati, Executive President, (Akhil Bhartiya Gujar Mahasabha), Padpadganj, New Delhi- 110091

AUTHENTICATED

The Above and below image show the representations against Jat inclusion from the Region of Delhi. Almost all members belong to some OBC community groups. Even those who came in individual capacity seem to be of OBC.

(61)  Shri Braham Prakash, General Secretary, (Delhi Ati Pichra Manch), New Delhi- 110082

(62)  Shri Braham Prakash, General Secretary, (Delhi Ati Pichra Manch), New Delhi- 110082

(63)  Shri R.P. Singh, 1337, Jud Bagh, Kotla Mubarak, New Delhi- 110003

(64)  Dr. P.C. Patanjali, President, (Pichra Varg Vikas Manch, Palam, New Delhi- 110045

(65)  Shri Krishan Kumar Arya, 333, Ishwar Colony, Bawana, Delhi- 110039

(66)  Akhil Bhartiya Vishwakarma Mahasabha.

(67)  Dr. Prem Chand Patanjali, President, (Pichra Varg Vikas Manch)

(68)  Shri Ombir Singh, OBC Reservation Raksha Samiti (Regd.)

(69)  Shri J.C. Gola (Pichra Varg Vikas Manch)


The next 5 images are of people who gave representations against the inclusion of Jat from the region of Haryana: (Please read 70 as 1 in the first representation)


HARYANA

## REPRESENTATIONS AGAINST INCLUSION OF JAT

By:-

(70)  Haryana Dakshini Lok Vikas Manch Rewari through Prof. Ranbir Singh Yadav

(2)  Kumhar Maha Sabha, Hisar through Col. OmPrakash (Retd.) Advocate, Hisar, Senior Vice President

(3)  Haryana Beragi Sabha Haryana (Regd.) by Virender Swami General Secretary

(4)  Most Backward Classes Federation of India through J.C. Gola, Chief General Secretary

(5)  Yuva Sain Samaj Sangathan Haryana

(6)  Pichra Varg Sangharsha Samiti, Sirsa through Gurdev Singh Rabi

AUTHENTICATED

(A.K. Manhotra)
Member Secretary

83

(7) Akhil Bhartiya Prajapati Kumhar Mahasangh
through Shri Shanta Kumar Arya, President

(8) Haryana Pradesh Pichra Varg (Block-A) Kalyan Samiti
through Shri Shanta Kumar Arya

(9) Yadav Samaj Sabha, Kurukshetra
through J.S. Yadav

(10) Jila Kumhar Sabha (Regd.), Sirsa

(11) Bharat Mukti Morcha
through Shri Subedar Purshottam, Vice President, Haryana.

(12) Yadav Sabha (Regd.) Chandigarh, Yadav Bhawan, Sec- 12.

(13) Jangid Brahmin Pradeshik Sabha, Haryana
through President Vidya Sagar Jangid

(14) Rohilla Tak Sabha (Regd.)
through Om Prakash Rohilla, President

(15) Pichra Varg Halka Safido

(16) Indira Panchal Rashtriya Rahul Gandhi Sangathan

(17) Dr. Ishwar Singh, Federation Backward Classes of Haryana.

(18) Shri Kishan Chand Panchal, Shri Vishwakarma Panchal Samaj
Sudhar    Sabha, Haryana.

(19) Haryana Backward Classes Federation, Rohtak.

(20) Jaswant Singh Panchal, Kamera Varg Kranti Morcha, Haryana
(21) Pichara Varg (A) Kalyankari Samiti, Haryana (Regd.)

(22) Rohilla Tak Sabha (Regd.)     AUTHENTICATED

84

~~through Balji Singh Kohlia & Om Prakash Kohlia~~

(23) Shri Vishwakarma Panchal Sabha Meham Chhoubisi, Rohtak.

(24) Pichara Varg Adhivakta Bar Association, Hisar

(25) Akhil Bhartiya Vishwakarma Panchal Mahasabha.

(26) Shri P.K. Kaushik, Haryana

(27) Shri Mahavir Singh Jangda (Deroliya), [Akhil Bhartiya Jangid Pradeshik Sabha, Haryana)

(28) Shri Om Prakash Verma (Pichra Varg Sangh Regd. No. 6251, Panipat)

(29) Shri Deshraj Verma S/o. Shri Sardara Ram (Haryana Kumhar Sabha, Barwala, Hisar)

(30) Shri Kashmir Chand Kamboj (Haryana Kamboj Sabha, Distt-Sirsa (Haryana) (Regd. No. 1177)

(31) Shri Rajender Tanwar, President (Shoshit Samaj, Haryana)

(32) Shri Ajit Jangda, (Vishwakarma Seva Samaj Samiti) (Regd No. 3003)

(33) Shri Virender Singh Bagoria (Haryana Kumhar Mahasabha) (Regd. No. 2105/99)

(34) Shri Ramratan Katasia, (Haryana Samajik Nyay Manch)

(35) Shri Subhash Chand Chechi & Baljit Singh Baisla (Akhil Bhartiya Veer Gujar Sabha, Haryana)

(36) Shri Subhash Jangda S/o. Shri Surajbhan Jangda, Shri Rajender Singh Kumhar & Man Singhbhar)

AUTHENTICATED

85

(37) Shri Ramkumar Ramba (Prajapati Jagrook Sabha, Haryana)

(38) Shri Ramkumar Ramba Prajapati (Haryana Pichra Varg
    Mahasabha)-

(39) Shri Tejbir Sain (Rashtriya Kranti Sena, Haryana)

(40) Shri Satyavan Verma, Mugalpura, Hisar, Haryana

(41) Shri Chhatarpal Soni, (Maharaja Ajmirh ji Swarnakar Vikas
    Trust, Tilak   Bazar, Talaki Gate, Hisar- 125001)

(42) Shri K.L.Chawla, (Punjabi Swabhiman Sabha, Rohtak- 124001,
Haryana)

(43) Shri Lakhiram Gangwa, (Kumhar Mahasabha), Hisar, Haryana

(44) Shri Rohtash Kumar Saini, (Saini Samaj), Sonepat, Haryana.

(45) Shri Ramsaroop Grover, (Sagar Jan Kalyan Seva Samiti), Rohtak
    (Regd.), Haryana.

(46) Shri Gagandeep Saini, (All India Saini Sewa Samaj), (Regd.),
    Gurgaon- 122001, Haryana.

(47) Shri Hitesh Saini, General Secretary (All India Saini Sewa Samaj
    (Regd.), Gurgaon- 122001, Haryana)

(48) Shri Prithvi Singh Kirodimal (Jila Kumhar Sabha, Sirsa,
Haryana)

(49) Rohilla Tak Sabha, (Reg. No. 757, Rohtak- 124001, Haryana)

(50) Shri Balbir Singh Prajapati S/o. Shri Kanhaiya Lal Prajapati,
    General Secretary, (Akhil Bhartiya Prajapati (Kumbhkar)
    Mahasangh, Haryana.    AUTHENTICATED

                                    (A.K. Sanghwa)                    86

(51) Shri Suresh Munjal, General Secretary, (Punjabi Sabha, Haryana (Regd.))

(52) Shri Satyavan Verma, Journalist, Ex. Sarpanch, Vill-Mugalpura, Distt- Hisar- 125113

(53) Shri Satbir Singh S/o. Shri Hawa Singh, (Pichra Varg Aarakshan Bachao Sangharsha Samiti),Israna (Panipat), Haryana.

(54) Shri Dhaniram Advocate, National President, (Akhil Bhartiya Dhobi Maha Samaj)

(55) Shri Bhup Singh Panchal, #645, Type-II, Panipat Thermal Colony, Asan- 132105

(56) Smt. Sushila W/o. Shri Mahipal. (Jogi Samaj Kalyanmanch, Israna, Panipat, Haryana)

(57) Kamera Varg Kranti Morcha, Jind, Haryana.

(58) Haryana Pradesh Saini Vikas Sabha, Panipat Road, Gohana.

(59) Shri Lal Bahadur Khowal, Advocate Distt Court, Hisar.

(60) Shri Manoj Kumar Vishwakarma

After Delhi and Haryana, we have the next two images showing the representations made against the Jat reservation from the Uttar Pradesh Region.

UTTAR PRADESH

**Representations Against Inclusion of JAT of Uttar Pradesh**

By:-

(71) KapilDev Arya (Sanyukt Samajvadi Dal)

(72) Nafiz Ahmed Salmani

(73) AtiPichara Varg Kalyan Samiti, Uttar Pradesh

(74) Shri Ram Singh Saini (Other Backward Classes)

(75) Shri Braham Singh Prajapati (Janadhikar Sangharsha Parishad)

(76) Shri Gajendra Pal Singh Prajapati & Tejpal Singh Saini (Ati Pichra Varg Sangharsha Samiti, Uttar Pradesh)

(77) Shri Janeshwar Dayal Tyagi

(78) Shri Than Singh, State General Secretary, (ST, SC, OBC officers Employee Mahasangh, Uttar Pradesh)

(79) Shri Pradeep Kumar Verma, General Secretary, (Shiva Sangh).

(80) Shri Anand Saini, Vill-Hansupura, P.O.-Noorpur, Bijnore, Uttar Pradesh.

(81) Shri Ram Singh Saini, Gajendra Pal Singh Prajapati (Ati Pichra Varg Sangharsha Samiti)

(82) Shri Tejpal Saini, Basantgarh, Shyohara, Bijnore (Ati Pichra Varg Sangharsha Samiti, Bijnore, Uttar Pradesh)

(83) Shri Gajendra Pal Singh Prajapati & Tejpal Singh Saini (Ati Pichra Varg Sangharsha Samiti, Uttar Pradesh)

AUTHENTICATED

(A.K. Mehrotra)

91

(84) Shri Gajendra Pal Singh Prajapati & Tejpal Singh Saini (Ati Pichra Varg Sangharsha Samiti, Uttar Pradesh)

(85) Shri Gajendra Pal Singh Prajapati & Tejpal Singh Saini (Ati Pichra Varg Sangharsha Samiti, Uttar Pradesh)

(86) Shri Gajendra Pal Singh Prajapati & Tejpal Singh Saini (Ati Pichra Varg Sangharsha Samiti, Uttar Pradesh)

(87) Shri Gajendra Pal Singh Prajapati & Ram Singh Saini (Ati Pichra Varg Sangharsha Samiti, Uttar Pradesh)

(88) Shri Braham Singh Prajapati (Janadhikar Sangharsha Parishad)

(89) Shri Fire Ram Prajapati (Rashtriya Ati Pichra Varg Mahasabha)

(90) Shri Bhanu Prasasd Kushwaha & Others

(91) Shri Gajendra Pal Singh Prajapati & Tejpal Singh Saini (Ati Pichra Varg Uthyan Samiti, Uttar Pradesh)

(92) Shri Amarpal Lodhi, Bulandsahar, Uttar Pradesh.

• If the names in list were enough to show the interests and imputed bias, the arguments forwarded by them show the actual and apparent bias in the whole activity. I have restricted my answers to few representations only. The reason for that is clearly visible in the kind of arguments given by them. If the NCBC and courts believe that these pedestrian arguments holds any ground, I wish them luck and hope that they should have some introspection to know that the more number of representations never means more arguments against a cause. E.g.

- In the first image we have a person named Tej Pal Singh Saini who is trying to show that 75% of posts in government services are taken by Jats in UP and Uttrakhand. But to support that claim neither he has shown any authentic report nor we have any government or media report available to prove his claims.

Power Corporation Ltd.(vs) Rajesh Kumar and others

(C.A. No.2608/2011 dated 27-4-2013) halsted quantified data.

3. Tej Pal Singh Saini, Chairman and

Shri Gajendra Pal Singh Prajapati, General Secretary

Ati Pichada Varg Utthan Samiti, Bijnore, U.P.

(i) In U.P. and Uttarakhand Jats are included in the respective State lists. After inclusion 75% of posts in Government Services are taken away by Jats. It really affects poor OBC people.

| Sl. No. | Reserve Post Name | No. of seats reserved for OBC | No. of Posts by JATs | No. of posts by Real OBC 78 Castes |
|---|---|---|---|---|
| 1 | B.T.C. Post for Baghpat Dist., 2010 | 27 | 21 | 6 |
| Sl. No. | Reserve Post Name | No. of seats reserved for OBC | No. of Posts by JATs | No. of posts by Real OBC 78 Castes |
| 2 | 2005-2010 District Panchayat Members in Meerut Dist. | 8 | 8 | 0 |
| 3 | 2005-2010 Block Chairman, Bijnore Dist. | 3 | 3 | 0 |
| 4 | Police recruitment 2010 | 9450 | 9031 | 419 |
| 5 | B.T.C. posts 2010 M.Nagar Dist. | 85 | 60 | 25 |
| 6 | B.T.C. posts 2010 Meerut Dist. | 218 | 119 | 99 |

AUTHENTICATED

If we closely observe the claim and try to find out the truth we will find that the claim has nothing to support it. E.g. What he is trying to show as BTC post, means Basic Teacher Certificate or Basic Training Certificate, an educational course made necessary for appointment as primary teacher in government schools. Overall UP has 75 districts but the person is so narrow minded that to support his claim he has data from 2-3 districts only, which are considered as Jat dominated regions of UP.

The colleges offering BTC course are not some IIT or IIM like educational centers that students from across the UP (forget about all India) are applying for them that can help in some conclusion.

According to careervendor.com, a website on information for education says that we have 34 BTC colleges in Meerut alone with 1800 seats.

Similarly, his claim on police recruitment is so big that one is forced to search as such things are always picked by media and often we have cases on it. E.g. in 2006 recruitment and in later recruitment of 2013 we have cases where CBI enquiries, protests and scams are reported. But strangely nothing is reported to show that the Jats selection was so high. It is nothing but a false claim which looks good on facebook or whatsapp circulation but too childish to be considered by government commissions and courts.

- After one frivolous representation we have a second person named Karan Singh Saini who tried to prove his point through some data. He is showing data from 2 districts and strangely in counter to the upper person the number of OBC people from other communities became high.

While, according to Tej Pal Singh Saini other OBC communities are unable to be recruited in the police because of jats but according to Karan Singh Saini when it comes to police force other OBC communities have higher number of people in duty.

The other message he want to convey is that by studying 2 districts of Western UP considered as Jat dominated we should make conclusions about whole of UP. These selective and subjective considerations with no data from government show that how much selective and frivolous these representations are. Add to that we need to know about the functioning of government organizations where people try to have posting in a town near to home. As Jat population is high in the Western UP it is understandable to have high numbers of Jat in these districts.

| | | | | | |
|---|---|---|---|---|---|
| 7 | B.T.C. posts 2010 Bijnore Dist. | 27 | 18 | 09 |

Jats are dominant in Politics, in the field of Education and Agricultur
They are not Socially or Educationally Backward.

4. Balraj, All India All India OBC Reservation Raksha Samiti, 246,

Sector-4 Vartalok, Vasundhara, Ghaziabad, UP.

(i) Inclusion of Jats in Central List will affect real Backward Class people like – Kumhar, Teli, Nai, Saini, Yadava, Gujjars, Sai Kurmi, Ansari, Kuresh, Vishwakarma, Pal and others throughout India.
(ii) Since Jats not attracted the criteria in Mandal Commission Report Jats are not included.

5. Karan Singh Saini, President, Ati Pichada Varg Sangharsh

Samiti, Moradabad, UP

(i) Jats are dominant in Western UP particularly in Moradabad, Bijnore,

Shahranpur, Sambhal, Meerut, Mathura, Agra etc.

(iii) Jats are lower than Brahmin and upper than other Backward

class people.

(iii) In UP Police Department in Rampur and Amroha Districts,

| | Total Police Appointed | Gen. | SC/ST | OBC | Jats |
|---|---|---|---|---|---|
| Rampur : | 1174 | 397 | 302 | 475 | 232 |
| Amroha : | 1200 | 268 | 342 | 590 | 302 |

*Most of the applicants insisted proper survey to find the status of Jats befo inclusion. All are stated Jats are not Socially opr Educationally Backwar Jats are powerful in politics, service, business and industries.*

*If Jats are included other OBCs will be totally affected.*

AUTHENTICATED

(A.K. Mangotra)

After these representations from UP which the NCBC considered as worth to be included we have some representations from Delhi. If the representations from UP wanted to have data from 2-3 districts should be compared to project the picture of whole UP, the representations from Delhi tried to compare the data from Delhi with All India Levels with global recommendations. E.g.

- Read the arguments given by Ombir Singh Mandar, an Advocate. When the total population of Delhi, as per 2011 census, was 1.67crore, he claims that Jat population was 2.7crore in Delhi and for all India it becomes 1.8%.

1) Shripal Saini, President, All India Saini Sewa Samaj, Delhi

2) Suman Saini, President, Apne Log Mahasangh, Delhi

(i) On 7.1.1995 Govt. of NCT of Delhi included number of castes in State Backward List. In that List Jats are not found place.
(ii) On 10-09-1993 R.N. Prasad notified various castes for inclusion from 14 States. In that also Jats not included.
(iii) Mandal Commission also not included Jats.
(iv) On 9-11-1990 NCBC rejected Jats. There is no substantive material produced before NCBC for review its order. As per Apex Court Judgement :
" P.N. Thakershi (vs) Pradhyam Singh ji" the Jats request for

review is not maintainable.

(v) Indian Institute of Public Administration Report dated 14-11-200 also not in favour of Jats.
3) Ombir Singh Mandar, Advocate, President, OBC Reservation Raksha Samiti, Delhi

(i) Population of Jats 2.7 crore in Delhi. 1.8% population all over Ind
(ii) 2006 BBC London declared Jats are forward.
(iii) As per recent Allahabad High Court Judgment those castes having sufficient

shares are to be excluded.

(iv) IAS in Rajasthan : 20, UP : 6, Haryana & Delhi : 41, Punjab : 5,

MP : 4

(v) Same manner IFS, IRS and allied service also.

(vi) During 2012 alone 30 Jats selected by UPSC.
(vii) Delhi Police 30%, Haryana Police 70%, Punjab Police 50%, Rajasthan Police 35% are Jats. It is above than population.
(viii) Jat Generals 14. Till not 20 Major Generals from Jats.
(ix) More awardees including Padma Awardees are Jats.
(x) More District and Additional District Judges Advocates are from

Jats.                                   AUTHENTICATED

It is understandable that what he wanted to show the 2.7crore for All India Level. What he wanted to convey was an all India population. But it definitely shows how serious the NCBC and Supreme Court was in formation and reading of report. It seems more like a friendly exercise where NCBC told others to say anything and we will publish. And later Judges instead of pointing it out said don't worry we will conclude on our own and will provide cover up to your report.

Otherwise no sane mind can digest his flimsy argument that in **2006 BBC declared Jat as forward** as argument against Jat reservation. See his other arguments made out of air with no data to support. Similarly, even if we take his figure of 2.7crore as the Jat population the all over India percentage comes out to be 2.23% based on 2011 census. It is only NCBC and courts who can show that his time-wasting arguments are given place in the report at first place.

Similarly, no government data says that 30 Jats are recruited in 2012. Still, the CSE-2012 had 998 candidates as selected and when we try to find out the percentage it comes out to be just 3%. If we had any authentic data on overall Jat population public (like SECC) then it will come out to be near that only.

Speakers, 13

Governors, 8 Ambassadors, MPs, MLAs, Corporators are Jats.

(xii) Delhi Police and Delhi Transport Corporation Jats are more in all levels.

(xiii) 61 Leading Actors, Models are Jats.

(xiv) More Academicians and Industrialists are from Jats.

4. R.P. Singh, Kotla Mubarakpur, Delhi

Survey Report submitted by D.K. Gandhi and Dr. B.K. Nagla is false report. Most of the applicants opposed Jats are rulers since from 18th Century. Dominant in Politics, Public Service and Business.

**HARYANA**

1. Shanta Kumar Arya, State President, Haryana Pradesh Pichda Varg

2) As per Article 340, Art.15(4), Art.16(4) Jats not eligible to include in the List of OBCs.
3) Social dominance, Educational, Economic, Political dominance of Jats
4) Large number of Jat Vice Chancellors, Academicians in Haryana and other States.
5) PM, Dy PM, CMs, MPs and MLAs in Jats
6) Civil Service, Police, Physical Education are occupied by Jats
7) Strongly opposing to include
8) Since 1913 Jats are running number of Schools, Gurukuls, Higher Educational Institutions and Professional Colleges. In the Edn. Institutions, they are appointing Jats and admitting Jat Students only

2. Prof. Ranveer Singh Yadav, Haryana Dakshina Lok Vikas Manch, Rewari Haryana.

(i) Haryana Jats not attracted the Parameters as per Art.16(4)

AUTHENTICATED

(A.K. Mangotra)
Member Secretary
National Commission for Backward Classes

98

But the frivolous ideas from this person doesn't stop here and he goes on spitting nonsense like 61 Leading Actors and Models are Jats, More Academicians and Industrialists are jats as if the whole exercise and report from NCBC is a joke rather than a serious discussion where we need to substantiate our claims also.

In that series we had another person named R P Singh from Delhi who felt that despite the Mughal dominance he had Jats as rulers in Delhi from 18th century.

**Representations from Haryana:**

In the above image on Delhi we had the start of representations from Haryana also where a person named Shanta Kumar was strongly opposing the inclusion of Jats but gives nothing factual to support his statements. E.g. In chapter 4 it was already discussed that how insignificant the education level in India and the Punjab region was. But for him Jats are running many colleges and schools since 1913.

The fact is that if he had some understanding on the articles 340, 15(4) and 16(4) of the constitution he might have understood that the articles also demand some universal and indisputable facts also to support any view. In India, while we have a lot of people from younger generation who are aware that how and why Ch. Charan Singh was made PM by Congress. People are aware that he is the only PM in India who never attended parliament as Prime Minister, as he never had the numbers.

But in this whole exercise of Jat reservation issue the old people who possibly be in the youth during Ch Charan Singh PM duration and were aware that he was popular as a Farmer leader, which even today forms nearly 50% of Indian population. In fact they are trying hard to show that he was just a caste leader or representative like them.

- After that a person called Ranveer Singh Yadav. While the person writes Prof. before his name but see the kind of superficial knowledge and arguments he has to give. As per Gurunam Singh Commission Report 1990 Jat representation was 17.82% but the population was 16% as per 1931 census.

In 1931 Haryana was part of Punjab province and the Punjab province included the West Punjab (which later became part of Pakistan) and East Punjab which is now an independent state. If despite them Jats had 16% of population then it gives a hint that how much Jat population is in State of Haryana and why the figure 17.82% was under-representation. The other argument is about Khap and Fatwa.

While I will deal about the Khaps in detail in the Book on Dharma but it is known to everyone that if in today's India anybody is considered as responsible even by courts, it is khap. It is this responsibility only that while courts will question them on some crimes and when despite the large number of crime of ideology opposite to the Khap ideas no court has idea that whom it should held responsible. These crimes become the crimes with no father or ideology behind.

(ii) As per Gurunam Singh Commission Report 1990, Jats represent 17.82% in Group A and B posts, whereas population is 16% as per 1931 census.

(iii) The Khap Panchyat issue Fatwas that cannot be changed by anybody.

(iv) They are ill treating Dalits and other OBCs.

3. Birendra Swamy, General Secretary, Haryana Bairagi Sabha, Rohtak, Haryana.

(i) In Haryana Assembly there are 27 Jat MLAs. Total MPs in Haryana 10. Jats 3

(ii) In 14th Common Wealth Games India won 32 Medals. Out of which 25 are by Jats.

4. Chander Bhan, Dy. P.A (Rtd.), Advocate, Hisar, Haryana

(i) During 1954 Punjab Govt. given 2% reservation to BCs. After formation of Haryana during 1966 the same continued for 67 BC castes (ii) 1979 BC Reservation was increased from 2% to 10%. On 1.1.79 Mandal Commission constituted and submitted its Report on 31.12.80 and recommended 27% to OBC. From 14-1-1980 till 1-12-89 that report was not implemented. When implemented during 1989 Jats opposed and burnt 300 buses in Haryana.

(iii) On 12-10-1993, Govt. of Haryana constituted second BC

Commission which recommended to include 5 castes namely

Ahirs, Gujjars, Mev, Lodh and Saini. For these 5 castes 11%

reservation recommended. 16% for remaining 67 castes.

(iv) Govt. of Haryana constituted Haryana BC Commission headed by Justice K.C. Gupta which recommended to include Jats, Jat Sikhs, Rors, Tyagis and Bisnois. It was opposed by all. Then the task of survey for 5 castes were given to the Centre for Research and Rural Industrial Development (CRRID), Chandigarh. Since its survey against to Jats Haryana Govt. changed and survey given to MD University, Rohtak and Prof. Dr. Khajan Singh Sangwan, HOD Sociology was appointed as Project Director. He is a Jat. The above Committee given false report. Based on the report K.C. Gupta Commission Report is false. Based on the above Commission Report, 2012 Haryana Govt. without including 27% Reservation, 10% reservation for above 5 castes

AUTHENTICATED

99

Now consider the arguments by other in that:

- One person named Birendra Swamy says that Jats won more medals so they need reservation. Those who quote Articles from Constitution should also know about the relation of sports with backwardness. For US, black people win many medals, does that mean that they are more developed than other people. Many African nations have a medal count more than many European and Asian nations including India. It is strange that despite so much aware citizens in India like them India still gives loan to them.

- Another person named Chander Bhan is trying hard to sound reasonable by providing selective information. E.g. While trying to display that because of Prof. K S Sangwan being Jat the committee report is false and illegal he forgets that the Mandal Commission based on whom people are enjoying reservation also belonged to a community which was made OBC by Mandal. The OBC Commission set by Haryana Government in 1990 under Justice Gurnam Singh had Sadhu Ram Saini as member and it recommended the inclusion of Jats and other communities also along with Saini and others, which K C Gupta commission also said to be included in OBC list.

It is only a biased exercise which can overlook those facts while trying to play that having a Jat as member for any commission for Jat reservation makes the report of commission illegal while forgets that the commission who gave them or other OBC people reservation also had members from the community who got reservation based on that report.

- Now consider the arguments given by another person named Chander Mal who feels that Haryana Assembly has 26 Jat MLAs while one person above felt it is 27.

- The next person named B R Verma seemed to be having data more than government that he knows the literacy status at community level without SECC, Transport companies, tenders awarded and property dealing reports based on which he came out with his trivial data and facts to give representation against Jat Reservation.

But the most pathetic thing is that no judge has shown the will to question those trivial arguments. The person named Chander Mal Sanujo had list of 96 Jats out of 197 HCS while the person next to him named B R Verma had 66 out of 220 HCS officers as Jats. This person doesn't stop here. He knows not just the ownership of registered companies but also of unregistered companies having Jat owner.

separately as a "Special Backward Class Reservation". It is illegal.

(v)Politically, Educationally, Economically, Industry, Sports, Cine

Field Jats in Haryana are dominant and powerful.

5. Chander Mal Sanujo, Secretary, Vishwa Karma Dharmsabha, Haryana

(i) Haryana BC Commission under the leadership of K.C. Gupta fixed social indicators=12, Educational Indicators=07, Economic Indicators=05 for 5 castes. Out of 12 indicators some are false, misleading and based on that reservation should not be given.
(ii) Total MPs from Haryana 10 among Jats 3 Total MLAs 90 Jats 26.
(iii) In IAS Total 176 Jats 41 (23.29%)
In HCS Total 197 Jats 96 (48.73%)

6. Dr. B.R. Verma, Gurgaon, Haryana

(i) Literacy Rate of Jats are high. Male 92% and Female 78%.
(ii)K.C. Gupta Commission Findings are false.
(iii )60% Transport, 65% Tenders in various Fields, 80% Property Dealin 50% Agencies are Jats.
(iii) 12250 Registered Large and Small Scale Industries and 5000 unregistered Industries in Haryana owned by Jats only.
(v) In State IPS Officers 105 out of it Jats 26

DSP 175 out of it Jats 70

IAS Promoters 45 out of it Jats 22

HCS 220 out of it Jats 66

DRO (Revenue) 27 out of it Jats 7

Thasildars 86 out of it Jats 36

Naib Thasildars 194 out of it Jats 96

In universities also Teaching and Non Teaching staffs are more than 50% are Jats.

The contention of 'Jat' caste/community people is that their main occupation is agriculture and similarly situated agricultures such as 'Yadvas, Kurmis, Gujjars and Lodhs' are included in the

AUTHENTICATED

100

Only a detailed discussion would have cleared the air on the sources of those frivolous facts submitted by the person. But our bad luck that we have courts who in the guise of Justice targets their hate and prejudices against Dharma. If someone had common sense than he must have asked this frivolous guy about the sources of his facts or the total numbers of the teaching and non teaching staff to gauge the sincerity of his claims.

But if those claims were not enough we had many more claims which will show that whole exercise was nothing but a joke. In the next image we have a written submission from a person named Ombir Singh in which he says that 2038 Head constables and 3753 Constables are posted in Delhi with various figures of representation based on caste-wise.

Reservation Raksha Samiti, represented by Shri Ombir Singh, President, the following information was furnished:

"From the information received from PIO-cum-Dy. Commissioner of Police (Security) HQ, and PIO/Asst. Commissioner of Police Traffic (HQ) Delhi, it is apparent that in the State of NCT of Delhi people of 'Jat' community are well placed and their representation in government services is substantive and even more than the ratio of their population.

Sl.No. Information

1. 2035 Head Constables and 3753 Constables are posted in Delhi Police.
2. The caste-wise details of Head Constables and Constables is as under:-

| Rank | Jat | Gujjar | Yadav |
|---|---|---|---|
| Head Constables | 647 (32%) | 72 (4%) | 28(1%) |
| Constables | 1185(32%) | 250(7%) | 22(1%) |

AUTHENTICATED

Now just visit the website of Delhi Police (http://www.delhipolice.nic.in/mobile/history.html) and read about its history. In 1951 the total strength of Delhi Police was 8000 personnel. If we add the numbers given by this person of police personnel it comes out to be 7000.

If we add the numbers from Traffic police and other clerks etc. given by him the figure will reach nearly to the 1961 strength of the Delhi Police, which was 12000. The present sanctioned strength is 83,762 with the number of people serving above 76000. If someone in NCBC or in Judiciary had used his common sense and searched the Delhi Police website the bluffs of NCBC reports can be caught easily.

But instead of doing the duty those institutions were busy in making people accept the other arguments like this population on total population of Jat, Gujjar and Yadav as if the Yadav and Gujjars from all India apply for the job in Delhi Police.

Also, while projecting those figures it is well known that except the Jats of Delhi and few parts of India, all other apply under open category and are selected under open category. While Yadav and Gujjars with whom he is trying to compare are eligible for open as well as OBC category reservation.

4. The caste-wise details of ASI/SI and Inspector is as under:

| Rank | Jat | Gujjar | Yadav |
|---|---|---|---|
| ASI | 169(27%) | 25(4%) | 19(3%) |
| SI | 193(42%) | 20(4%) | 09(2%) |
| Inspector | 20(25%) | 01(1%) | 01(1%) |

5. 28 ACPs, 02 Addl. DCPs, 02 Addl. CSP and 01 Joint CP are posted.

6. The caste-wise details of ACP/DCPs is as under:

| Rank | Jat | Gujjar | Yadav |
|---|---|---|---|
| ACP | 05(18%) | 00 (Nil) | 00(Nil) |

B. In the Traffic Department of Delhi Police (As per letter No.F.935/RTI/13/5228/RTI Cell/Tr. Dated 21-11-2013)

| Ranks | Jat community | Gujjar community | Yadav community |
|---|---|---|---|
| H.Constables | 323 | 77 | 99 |
| Constables | 1405 | 259 | 467 |

S.No. Information

1. 201 ASI, 187 SI & 64 Inspectors

2. The caste-wise details of ASI, SI & Inspector is as under:

| Rank | Jat | Gujjar | Yadav |
|---|---|---|---|
| ASI | 24(12%) | 8(4%) | 9(4%) |
| SI | 12(7%) | 4(2%) | 6(4%) |
| Inspectors | 13(20%) | 2(1%) | 3(1%) |

AUTHENTICATED

Adding to that we have 1931 census where it was clearly mentioned that in terms of being local to Delhi it was Jats who had importance in 225 villages in comparison to the figure of 70 villages with Gujjar and 35 villages with Yadav as main community.

In fact, we had many more things to discuss not just the facts and figures given in this book. Only when you have an objective discussion these things and many more things come out. But, it is the nature of the forces of Adharma to feel that whatever knowledge they have is the complete knowledge and nothing in this world exist outside that. Some other figures are given to show those frivolous arguments before I move to the conclusions from NCBC and show the biased personalities present in the whole decision-making process.

...... ..............

1. 16 ACPs, 07 DCPs

2. The caste-wise details of ACPs, DCPS is as under:

| Rank | Jat | Gujjar | Yadav |
|---|---|---|---|
| ACP | 05 (30%) | 01(6%) | 01(6%) |
| DCP | ---- | 01 | ---- |

The PIO/Dy. Commissioner of Police, 3rd BN, DAP, Delhi Police, Vikas Puri Police Complex ND vide his letter No.2158/RTI Cell (ID-319)/13/3rd Bn., DAP dated 26-11-2013 has also forwarded the relevant information under RTI which are summarized as under:-

TOTAL STRENGTH:

| | | |
|---|---|---|
| i) | Constables | 1319+101 = 1420 |
| ii) | H/Clerk | 472+11 = 483 |
| iii) | ASI | 21+14 = 35 |
| iv) | SI | = 35 |
| v) | Inspector | = 18 |

| POST | JAT COMMUNITIES | GUJJAR COMMUNITIES | YADAV |
|---|---|---|---|
| Constable | 499(39%) | 42 (30%) | 218(17%) |
| H/Constable | 168(36%) | 06(1%) | 58(13%) |
| ASI | 20(57%) | 01(3%) | 06(16%) |
| SI | 11(31%) | 00(NIL) | 03(8%) |
| Inspector | 03(16%) | 00(NIL) | 00(NIL) |

Above figures are more relevant in comparison of their ratio of their population:-

JAT population    AUTHENTICATED    2.7 Crores

(A.K. Malhotra)

309

Gujjar Population                     3.65 Crores

Yadav Population                      13.7 Crores

Additionally following information is relevant to understand the effect of grant of reservation in States where people of Jat community have almost consumed substantive number of seats in OBC quota whereby they have made the purpose of reservation for OBCs defeated. Following are some examples:

R.A.S. (Rajasthan Administrative Services Class I Post)

JAT included in State OBC List in the year 2001 (From 2001 to 2011)

Total OBC candidates selected                    30

JAT candidates selected                          25

Others                              05

In State of Uttar Pradesh where Jat is included in the State List of OBC following information reveals that they have occupied most of the OBC seats.

State BTC (Primary Teacher) Selection 2010 (Muzaffar Nagar)

i)  Total candidates selected under OBC          85
ii) Candidates from JAT community                60
iii)Others                                       25

State BTC-2010 (Basic Teachers Course) Selection in District Baghpat (UP)

Total OBC seats                                  27

Candidates from JAT community selected           21

Others                              AUTHENTICATED         06

(A.K. Mahajntra)

106

| | |
|---|---|
| Total OBC candidates | 27 |
| JATs selected | 18 |
| Others | 09 |

Besides it is further submitted that the people of Jat community have performed much better than those of other castes and have got selected in prestigious civil services which is much higher than the number proportionate to their population. In UPSC Civil Services Examination of 2012 the number of people belonging to Jat caste selected is 30 out of total 998 candidates from all over India.

Besides the member of Jat community has outstanding representation in Politics, Cinema, academics, sports, administration, judiciary, army, air force etc.

**Speaker Lok Sabha**

(1)   Dr. Balram Jakkar

(2)   Shri Ram Niwas Mirdha (Dy. Chairman, Rajya Sabha)

(3)   Sardar Gurdial Singh Dhillon

**Governors:**

(1)   Dr. Sarup Singh

(2)   Balram Jakhar

(3)   Virender Verma

(4)   Sultan Singh

(5)   Randhir Singh

(6)   Mrs. Kamla Beniwal

(7)   Dr. Har Swarup Singh

AUTHENTICATED

(A.K. Mangotra)
Member Secretary
National Commission for Backward Classes

102

(8) Mrs. Chandra Vati Beniwal

(9) Sardar Surjit Singh Barnala

(10) Joginder Singh

(11) Har Charan Singh Brar

(12) M.S.Randhawa

(13) Chief Marshal Arjun Singh

## Ambassadors

(1) Kanwar Natwar Singh

(2) Dr. Har Swarup Singh

(3) BNhagwan Singh

(4) Maharaja Yadvender Singh

(5) M.C.M. Arjun Singh

(6) Maj. T.S.Bal

(7) G.S.Chhattarwal

(8) Shri Ajay Singh

## Chief Ministers

| | | |
|---|---|---|
| (1) | Chaudhary Charan Singh | U.P. |
| (2) | Chaudhary Bansi Lal | Haryana |
| (3) | Chaudhary Dev. Lal | Haryana |
| (4) | Chaudhary Hukum Singh | Haryana |
| (5) | Shri Om Prakash Chautala | Haryana |
| (6) | Shri Bhupinder Singh Hooda | Haryana |
| (7) | Dr. Sahib Singh Verma | Delhi |
| (8) | Mrs. Vasundhra Raje (married to a Jat) | Rajasthan |
| (9) | Sardar Partap Singh Kairon | Punjab |
| (10) | Sardar Darbara Singh | Punjab |

AUTHENTICATED

108

92

(11) Sardar Lachman Singh Gill                     Punjab "

47. All India OBC Reservation Raksha Samiti, a registered society, filed objections dated 24-2-2014 for inclusion of the Jats in the Central List of OBCs in addition to the earlier representations filed by them submitting further material stating that the Jats have a Website viz. "www.Jat Forum.com.," and a perusal of the said Website reveals the particulars of the Jat Officers in various services, highly dignified occupations/employment position, etc.

48. One Mr.Praveen Kumar Soni S/o. Shri Jagdish Prasad Soni of Bhiwani, Haryana gave a detailed representation dated 24-2-2014 objecting the inclusion of the Jats enclosing twelve annexures and in the said representation/objection, it is stated that the interference of the Government driving the NCBC to submit its report in favour of the Jats for their inclusion in the Central List of OBCs based on the reports, material and representation is against the spirit of the Constitution of India and is nothing but a political compulsion because the Jat caste is not entitled for their inclusion in the List of OBCs. It is further stated that it is also against the decision of the Supreme Court in the case of Indra Sawhney Vs. Union of India. As per the said judgment, certain objective social and other criteria has to be satisfied before any group or class of citizens could be treated as backward. If the executive includes, for collateral reasons, groups or classes not satisfying the relevant criteria, it would be a clear case of fraud on power.

The action is also against the view taken by the Supreme Court in the case of M.Nagarajan and Ashok Kumar Thakur case. The

AUTHENTICATED

agitations of 'Jat' community and violent protests that is causing loss to private and public property, and disruption of the free flow of essential goods of life. Such a practice is unconstitutional, arbitrary and unreasonable. The political and illegal pressure of the 'Jat' community is forcing the Government to act against the law and infringing the fundamental rights of other backward classes. Jats are represented adequately in the public employment and in the politics also. The 'Jat' caste/community do not deserve to be included in the Central List of OBCs as they are not socially, educationally and economically backward. Jats are having high status in the villages and towns and they are addressed as Choudhary and even the lady belonging to the Jat community is being called as Choudharan in Haryana. 96% people belonging to Jat community have got agriculture holding which is a symbol of high status, as the price of agriculture land at present had arisen many folds, starting from Rs. 50 lakhs to 2 crore per acre. The social status of the Jats could be gauged from the fact that they do not cultivate the lands themselves but get it cultivated by engaging labour from other backward classes. Out of 90 MLAs in Haryana, 27 M.L.As. belong to Jat community (29% of the total population that is much more than their percentage of population). From Haryana, there are three Lok Sabha Members and one Rajya Sabha member. There are 168 Officers under IAS cadre in Haryana and out of 168, 72 belong to Haryana domicile and 96 belong to the other States. Thus the representation of Jat IAS Officers is 39% in Haryana. In Haryana, there are 19 Jat IPS Officers. There are 13 IFS Officers from the Jat community. There are 70 Jat Officers in the Higher

AUTHENTICATED

[A. K. Mangotra]

The names given as the people with high posts look good as long as we are guided by our narrow and subjective biases. The moment we start looking at the total number of people who served as Governor, Ambassadors almost all figures comes to normal and below normal. But the neglect of those considerations by people who claim to hold the responsibility of Justice and equality in India shows that how much impression they have of ideologies and feelings that they accepted those pedestrian claims.

And if those claims were not enough we had the conclusions or recommendations of NCBC which are as pedestrian as the whole exercise was. E.g.

- In below image NCBC is talking about a flaw that the comparable studies of other OBC communities was not done. Now consider this argument with the criteria of the Mandal commission, given as the next figure and tell me one criterion in that which says that you need to have comparable figures from other OBC communities.

(iv)    The biggest flaw which came out during the examination of the report by NCBC and subsequently highlighted during the Public Hearing was that the MDU study was very selective ( allegedly deliberately ? ) in nature. The MDU study collected data on 27 Social Indicators,12 Educational Indicators and 10 Economic indicators. These were compared across 16 castes and rankings were given to each caste based on their performance on each of these indicators. The final outcome of the Survey was based on the aggregate of these ranking figures. Very tellingly, out of the 16 castes studied in this survey, 5 castes were those under present consideration and out of the remaining 11 castes, there were no castes examined which are considered comparable to Jats namely - the comparable figures for Ahirs, Yadavas, Kurmis and Gujars (which are otherwise said to be comparable OBCs and predominantly land owning communities) have not been studied at all for any of the Social, Educational or Economic parameters either in the MDU Report or in the Commission's report. Jats have been compared mostly with Rajputs, Bhramins, Maithili, Goswami, Gaur, Panjabi, Vaish which are traditionally considered as forward castes. Their comparision with other OBCs like Gujars, Ahirs, Yadavas and Kurmis is sorely lacking thus leaving a very big question mark on the selective collection of data by the Surveying agency. During the Public Hearing, many presenters pointed this out that if they are compared with these groups, the Jats will be seen to be superior. The outcome of the Survey was thus a foregone conclusion.

It is only the first criteria where you need to take the views of higher communities, barring that all other things can be done by using the state figures and comparing that with the figures of the community under consideration, as all are in comparison to the state average.

## A. Social

(i)     Castes/Classes considered as socially backward by others.

(ii)    Castes/Classes which mainly depend on manual labour for their livelihood.

(iii)   Castes/Classes where at least 25% females and 10% males above the State average get married at an age below 17 years in rural areas and at least 10% females and 5% males do so in urban areas.

(iv)   Castes/Classes where participation of females in work is at least 25% above the State average.

## B. Educational

(v)     Castes/Classes where the number of children in the age group of 5-15 years who never attended school is at least 25% above the State average.

(vi)    Castes/Classes where the rate of student drop-out in the age group of 5-15 years is at least 25% above the State average.

(vii)   Castes/Classes amongst whom the proportion of matriculates is at least 25% below the State average.

## C. Economic

(viii)  Castes/Classes where the average value of family assets is at least 25% below the State average.

(ix)    Castes/Classes where the number of families living in Kuccha houses is at least 25% above the State average.

(x)     Castes/Classes where the source of drinking water is beyond half a kilometer for more than 50% of the households.

(xi)    Castes/Classes where the number of households having taken consumption loan is at least 25% above the State average.

If that was not enough then consider this argument by NCBC of violation of "Nemo Judex In Re Sua" (Next Figure). If the K C Gupta Commission report was in violation of this principle then which principle was violated by Mandal Commission report? Whether it was Mandal as member of the OBC Commission or the members in the other commissions set in the state of Haryana and others for reservation, all had members from community which got reservation.

Not only that even the constitutional bodies like National Commission for Scheduled Castes, National Commission for Scheduled Tribes or the statutory commissions like National Commission for Women, National Commission for Minorities have chairman or members who are always in violation of the principle of "Nemo Judex In Re Sua", but no judge, media or commission ever said that it is in violation of this principle.

(a) Apart trom Justice K.C. Gupta, the other Members of the Commission were Shri Jai Singh Bishnoi, Shri Som Dutt, Advocate, Shri Arjun Dev Gulati, Shri Rao Ranpal Singh and Shri Telu Ram Jangra. It is seen that Shri Bishnoi belongs to Bishnoi caste and Shri Som Dutt is a Ror. In other words, in the Commission, two of the Members had interests in the outcome of the case since Bishnoi and Ror castes were under consideration and thus the composition was not following one of the cardinal principals of Natural Justice which says - "Nemo Judex In Re Sua". A man shall not be judge in his own cause. The Report gave OBC status (albcit "Special") to Rors and Bishnois along with three other castes including Jats. Speaker after speaker after gave vent to this allegation of bias during the Public Hearing.

(b) Not only this, it is also seen that the report of the Justice K.C Gupta Commission was primarily based on the survey conducted in the year 2012 by the MDU, Rohtak. The project was implemented by the single Project Director, a retired Prof. K.S. Sangwan. Incidentally, he is also belonging to the Jat community. The Vice Chancellor of the MDU, Rohtak during the concerned period was Prof. R.P. Hooda who is also a Jat. All of them were accused of bias in the whole survey and subsequent report during the Public Hearings held in Delhi.

(vi) The survey was conducted among 49,817 households belonging to 16 castcs drawn from all the Districts of Haryana. Interestingly, the comparable figures for Ahirs, Yadavas, Kurmis and Gujars (which are otherwise said to be comparable OBC communities) have not been studied for any of the Social, Educational or Economic parameters either in the MDU Report or in the Commission's report. During the Public Hearing, many presenters pointed this out that if they are compared with these groups, the Jats will be seen to be superior. The Survey compared the Jats mostly with higher castes like Bhramins, Rajputs, Punjabis, Vaish, Gaur etc which are in any case higher classes.

(a)    Apart from Justice K.C. Gupta, the other Members of the Commission were Shri Jai Singh Bishnoi, Shri Som Dutt, Advocate, Shri Arjun Dev Gulati, Shri Rao Ranpal Singh and Shri Telu Ram Jangra. It is seen that Shri Bishnoi belongs to Bishnoi caste and Shri Som Dutt is a Ror.   In other words, in the Commission, two of the Members had interests in the outcome of the case since Bishnoi and Ror castes were under consideration and thus the composition was not following one of the cardinal principals of Natural Justice which says - "Nemo Judex In Re Sua". A man shall not be judge in his own cause. The Report gave OBC status (albeit "Special") to Rors and Bishnois along with three other castes including Jats. Speaker after speaker after gave vent to this allegation of bias during the Public Hearing.

(b) Not only this, it is also seen that the report of the Justice K.C Gupta Commission was primarily based on the survey conducted in the year 2012 by the MDU, Rohtak.  The project was implemented by the single Project Director, a retired Prof. K.S. Sangwan. Incidentally, he is also belonging to the Jat community. The Vice Chancellor of the MDU, Rohtak during the concerned period was Prof. R.P. Hooda who is also a Jat. All of them were accused of bias in the whole survey and subsequent report during the Public Hearings held in Delhi.

(vi)    The survey was conducted among 49,817 households belonging to 16 castes drawn from all the Districts of Haryana. Interestingly, the comparable figures for Ahirs, Yadavas, Kurmis and Gujars (which are otherwise said to be comparable OBC communities) have not been studied for any of the Social, Educational or Economic parameters either in the MDU Report or in the Commission's report. During the Public Hearing, many presenters pointed this out that if they are compared with these groups, the Jats will be seen to be superior. The Survey compared the Jats mostly with higher castes like Bhramins, Rajputs, Punjabis, Vaish, Gaur etc which are in any case higher classes.

But how can they say this. This principle which is now projected as being violated is the principle which is practiced all along by them. E.g. Under Justice Ranganath Mishra we had a commission named as "National Commission for Linguistics and Religious Minorities" and the members of that commission were-Tahir Mahmood, Anil Wilson and Mohinder Singh. Similarly, we had Sachar Committee under Justice Rajinder Sachar and most of the members were from the community for which it was formed.

We have Press Council of India to keep control over the activities of Press. But the same has big list of members from Press. The moment government tries to have control over media they will claim to have self-regulation.

- Another observation from NCBC says that the KC Gupta Commission hasn't studied the representation of Jats in Armed Forces.

(viii) While highlighting the fact that the Jats are not proportionately represented in the Government Services, the survey has forgotten (deliberately ?) to study the representation of Jats in the Armed Forces of the Union. What has only been studied is Direct Civil and Allied Services and Class I, II, III and IV Govt Services and the representation of Jats in these services. It is well-known that Jats, both Sikhs and Hindus, are among the communities well-represented in the Armed Forces including the officer categories. In the North-Western States, military service has been enjoying a higher level of preference and prestige. One would have expected that the Haryana Backward Classes Commission which has given as many as 37 tables apart from the Annexures, to give also statistics of representations of different communities in the Armed Forces, particularly in the officer categories. Its omission cannot be rationally explained and it can be presumed that if those statistics had been given, the case of the Jats of Haryana for inclusion in the

If we look at KC Gupta Commission, we will find that the commission was set by the Government of Haryana for the study of Haryana. If under that Terms of Reference the commission doesn't include the central government service then it is understandable to a neutral person.

Only a person with subjective mindset can claim it as an error. Because if it was required then we should also know that the study should have involved all the central government services. People join Army as a representative of India not that of Haryana or other region. These arguments by NCBC not just show that how much ridiculous they were in their analysis but also the sense of lack of national considerations prevalent among them.

But people for whom representation in Police means representation in Whole Delhi Government services, it was natural to conclude that representation in Armed Forces mean representation in all other central government services. They consider those points as valid points while deliberately forgetting the terms of reference of the commission and the service categories which should be studied. E.g. In all the Central Government Services Jats have only Armed Forces as option where the competition is fare. While all other Central Government jobs have reservation because of which the members from other communities get jobs. So, if you study them the claims of high representation will start falling apart and under that situation the Judges will require more efforts toward Adharma to make the report acceptable to all.

It is well-known that Jats, both Sikhs and Hindus, are among the communities well-represented in the Armed Forces including the officers categories. In the North-Western States, military service has been enjoying a higher level of preference and prestige. One would have expected that the Haryana Backward Classes Commission which has given as many as 37 tables apart from the Annexures, to give also statistics of representations of different communities in the Armed Forces, particularly in the officer categories. Its omission cannot be rationally explained and it can be presumed that if those statistics had been given, the case of the Jat of Haryana for inclusion in the list of Backward Classes would have completely fallen".

(iv) "It is also difficult to believe that a larger number of percentage of Jat perceived themselves as Backward Classes than do Scheduled Castes."

If someone is so tempted to do that then NCBC was the best organization to do that. Why doesn't it called the data from all the PSUs, Ministries of Central Government and other jobs so that it can have the complete study.

While National Sample Survey Organization (NSSO) 70th Survey shows that 45.4% of all landholdings (with 52% of Large Holding) belongs to the OBC Community as identified by the Mandal Commission, but as per NCBC Mandal never meant to have agriculture to be considered as the manual labor. But instead of questioning those arguments with facts we have judges who consider those arguments (with no facts to support as the binding arguments and the arguments which need to be propagated.

10. Similarly, there is a complete misinterpretation of the term "Manual Labour for their livelihood" which is the second criteria of Social backwardness evolved by the NCBC and based on the Mandal Commission Report. The MDU survey (and the resultant K.C. Gupta Commission Report) has found that a vast majority of Jats are involved in "Manual labour for their livelihood". What has not been

AUTHENTICATED

brought out or attempted to be ascertained in the questionnaire is whether the Jats are working on their land or are they working on someone else's land as daily labourers? The survey clearly brings out that the Jats are a land owning community and it would be all but natural that they would be putting their labour on their own land to the extent possible. In addition they would be hiring manual labourers from oouside. But, this is not to say that they are performing manual labour for others as their source of their daily livelihood. What the Mandal Commission said was that those classes are backward which take up manual labour for their livelihood and work as labourers in lands belonging to someone else. This has been completely misinterpreted by the MDU Survey as also the State Commission and all the Jats have been shown as Manual Labourers.

What the K.C. Gupta Commission should have done was to try and ascertain whether the Jats work as manual labourers on someone else's land or not. Then possibly the real picture of Backward Classes could have emerged. During our Public Hearings we asked many people (both 'for' and 'against') whether a significant proportion of Jats work as labourers on somebody else's fields. The reply was a resounding 'no'. All stated that they either work on their land or do some other non-manual work. They never work as manual labourers for their day to day living on somebody else's land. As such this second important aspect of the National Backward Classes Commission's criteria for determining backwardness was virtually misinterpreted by the MDU survey first and subsequently by the K.C. Gupta Commission's Report also. Jats working in the area of agriculture on their own fields has been taken as "Manual Labour" in the MDU survey whereas it was reaffirmed during the Public Hearings that most of the Jats are land-owning (87% as per MDU report) and they never do manual labour on anyone else's field. A rare case may be a Jat who will go to a far off place to do manual

Add to that we have the same NCBC Commission who when rattled by DoPT consideration of Creamy Layer said that the income criteria is not applicable for Salary or Agriculture Income. As OBC reservation is not for Agriculture community why the commission is worried about 6lakh (now 8lakh) income criteria used for agriculture.

When it comes to the interests of present OBC communities those Retired High Court judges who say that even the sons of PSUs CEO are eligible for reservation and when it comes to other communities even a farmer with 2-3 hectares of land is not eligible based on the revised meaning of Mandal criteria. Only a biased judge can support that argument and the same was displayed in the judgment (Para 52) as:

60

at "not less than 52%" (***Indra Sawhney***) certainly must have gone up considerably as over the last two decades there has been only inclusions in the Central as well as State OBC Lists and hardly any exclusion therefrom. This is certainly not what has been envisaged in our Constitutional Scheme.

**52.** In so far as the contemporaneous report for the State of Haryana is concerned, the discussion that has preceded indicate adequate and good reasons for the view taken by the NCBC in respect of the said Report and not to accept the findings contained therein. The same would hardly require any further reiteration.

If that is not enough, consider the observations of NCBC on Hukam Singh Committee of 2001 where the commission is of the view that the commission report being 14 years old is not suitable for consideration.

### Social Justice Committee Report: Uttar Pradesh (2001)

This is a major report emanating from Uttar Pradesh State in the year 2001 which was listed amongst the 8 documents placed before the Group of Minister (GOM) Meeting. ICSSR has also examined this committee report.

2.     The Committee was also popularly known as the Hukam Singh Committee    and is today 14 years old thereby having a time

AUTHENTICATED

123

(A. K. Mangotra)

limitation on the available data sets.   It was a three Member committee set up under Shri Hukam Singh, Minister of Uttar Pradesh and having Shri Ramapati Shastri, Minister and Shri Daya Rampal, MLA as Members.   However, this committee has neither studied all the social educational aspects of the Jat community and nor was it confined to be a study of OBC castes of Uttar Pradesh. The primary objective of this committee was to investigate all projects, organizations and facilities extended to SCs/STs and OBCs in the State of U.P.   Another objective was to propose necessary alteration in the reservation for SCs/STs and OBCs   after the formation of Uttaranchal State. The committee was also required to propose probable alterations in the SC/ST and OBC quota for the truncated State of UP.

Now consider the views of NCBC on the book of K.L. Sharma, based on the collection of 1987 essays with one essay which detailed about the Akbar time i.e. nearly 400 plus years old data or facts.

... Caste and Class in India – K.L. Sharma (ED-1994)

This twenty year old book listed in the GOM meeting is a collection of 20 papers which were presented in a national seminar conducted by the Training for Development Scholarship Society (Pune) in December, 1987. The papers cover the complex dynamics of the nexus between caste and class in different States of India. The collection of articles highlights the fact that caste and class are inseparable aspects of India's social formation. However, the dynamics of the game varies from region to region and U.P is the subject matter of only one chapter with the Heading "Caste, Land and Political power in U.P" (written by Shri Imtiaz Ahmad and Dr NC Saxena).

2.    This paper ( the only one on UP ) goes into the historical proportion of numbers of castes in U.P and the Jats have been listed as land owning castes along with the Brahmins and Tyagis. During the time of Akbar the Jats formed 20% of the revenue source of Agra District. However, the collapse of the Central Moghul Authority laid down the path for land control by caste groups like Jats, Gujars and Tyagis in the districts of upper Doab. The British policy was to protect the old hereditary peasantry in the position of their ancestral states.

3.    After studying various aspects, the paper finally goes on to say how the Zamindari system was abolished and how various
AUTHENTICATED
Governments tried to introduce reservations to benefit their constituencies. On the issue of Jats, this paper concludes that "the intermediate caste in U.P can be broadly divided into three categories; i.e. Jats, Tyagis, Bhumihars, who have a considerable position in land, possess high ritual status and because of their regional concentration are dominant in the politics of a few districts". From this reading of the paper itself, it is clear that this study certainly does not categorize Jats into the backward classes. If anything, it only reaffirms their dominant position in the society based on their land power and their numerical strength in the areas under West UP.

But in words of NCBC this 400 year old data set has no time limitation on the data sets and reinforces the findings of the NCBC. This selective interpretation shows the level of prejudices and biases prevalent in the NCBC and by supporting those arguments without challenging the findings Supreme Court judges has shown that how much actual and apparent bias was needed to approve and make the NCBC report as mandatory to follow.

That approval is clearly visible from the Judgment where the judges recognized the importance given by NCBC to the K L Sharma report

**37.** The statistics and data available in the book – Caste and Class in India by K.L. Sharma are of considerably old vintage. The book, itself, is 20 years old. In any case, in the said book it has been recorded that *"the intermediate caste in U.P. can be broadly divided into three categories i.e. Jats, Tyagis, Bhumihars, who have a considerable position in land, possess high ritual status and because of their regional concentration are dominant in the politics of a few districts".* The aforesaid view was specifically taken note of by the NCBC while tendering its advice to the Government.

But Judges for Jat Reservation kept repeating that we need more present data to uphold the Jat reservation as the community had the backwardness based on a 1980's criteria in start of 21st century, but still India is progressing and a decade old data seems to be too old. A nation which is so dynamic where whole reservation is projected as based on historical deprivations. A nation where the Socio-Economic Caste Census Data which was collected in 2011 and finally compiled in 2014 is yet to be made public after nearly 5 years of completion.

Still a decade old data is too much while we can make conclusions on the 400 hundred years old data and on 1931 census etc. if it comes to the interests of the NCBC and the decision-makers.

the required scrutiny. Proceeding on that basis what is clear is that save and except the State Commission Report in the case of Haryana (Justice K.C. Gupta Commission Report) which was submitted in the year 2012, all the other reports as well as the literature on the subject would be at least a decade old. The necessary data on which the exercise has to be made, as already observed by us, has to be contemporaneous. Outdated statistics cannot provide accurate parameters for measuring backwardness for the purpose of inclusion in the list of Other Backward Classes. This is because one may legitimately presume progressive advancement of all citizens on every front i.e. social, economic and education. Any other view would amount to retrograde governance. Yet, surprisingly the facts that stare at us indicate a governmental affirmation of such negative governance inasmuch as decade old decisions not to treat the Jats as backward, arrived at on due consideration of the existing ground realities, have been reopened, inspite of perceptible all round development of the nation. This is the basic fallacy inherent in the impugned governmental decision that has been challenged in the present proceedings. The percentage of the OBC population estimated

- If that was not enough then consider this observation on education:

**68.** In so far as their educational backwardness is concerned, it is stated by them that there are more dropouts at the high school level and there is less women education. But it is the contention of the Objectors that the 'Jats' are rich having large agricultural land holdings and owners of the buildings and the affluent 'Jats' are satisfied with the school education to engage themselves to look after their estates, agricultural lands and urban properties. The dropouts of 'Jats' in the high school level is not because of the poverty but for the reason that they are affluent to take care of their own family properties. It is further stated that 'Jats' women also got good education compared to other developed backward classes.

While all other communities have a dropout because of lack of money but when it comes to Jat we have NCBC, who because of negligence or subjective biases in the judiciary can get any falsehood accepted. This falsehood has now started to touch the heights and the dropout because of being affluent not poverty is the just one aspect of that.

- The next is this Fiji Argument where if someone who went away long back from India and became Prime Minister of a small Foreign nation, it becomes a reason to show the progress of the community in India.

13.     The NCBC is certainly not convinced by this facetious argument of the State Commission which only strengthens the feeling of doubt and bias in the Report which was amply highlighted during the Public Hearing. During the Public Hearing, people rose up to say that Jats have been Prime Ministers of not only India ( Ch Charan Singh ), they have even ruled abroad as the PM of Fiji.

And this lack of regard for equality was also showed and written by the judges in their judgment. The judges made it clear that for Jat reservation you need to have more than just to show that you are equivalent to the rest of OBC communities.

backwardness must also cease to be relative; possible wrong

inclusions cannot be the basis for further inclusions but the

gates would be opened only to permit entry of the most

distressed. Any other inclusion would be a serious abdication

of the constitutional duty of the State. Judged by the aforesaid

standards we must hold that inclusion of the politically

organized classes (such as Jats) in the list of backward classes

mainly, if not solely, on the basis that on same parameters

other groups who have fared better have been so included

cannot be affirmed.

In fact, the judges were so biased in their decision making that many states like Bihar, Gujarat, Madhya Pradesh etc. which had no or very little discussion in the report were also concluded by the judges as being adequately covered and proven by NCBC that the decision was not biased:

21. The decisions in *Barium Chemicals Ltd. Vs. Company Law Board*[2]; *Rohtas Industries Ltd. Vs. **S.D. Agarwal & Ors.**[3]; **Shri Sitaram Sugar Co. Ltd. & Anr.** Vs. **Union of India & Ors.**[4] and **Gazi Saduddin** Vs. **State of Maharashtra & Anr.**[5] have been relied upon to contend that the satisfaction of the Central Government is open to challenge and within the reach of the judicial scrutiny both on grounds of its legal fragility and ex facie unreasonableness. Learned counsel for the petitioners has very elaborately taken us through the advice/report of the NCBC dated 26.02.2014 to contend that the exhaustive report of the said body contain a detailed analysis of the facts recorded in the reports of the various State Commissions. The said exercise clearly demonstrates that the Jats are a forward community in all the States in question. The contrary view of the Union

## The Actual and Apparent Bias of Judges

**Actual Bias** is the kind of bias where the decision-maker in the exercise was prejudiced in favor of or against a party. And, **Apparent Bias** is the kind of bias where a judge or other decision-maker is not a party to a matter and does not have an interest in its outcome, but through his or her conduct or behavior gives rise to a suspicion that he or she is not impartial.

In the Writ Petition Civil 274 of 2014 we had two judges with one having an actual bias and the other joined the forces of Adharma because of his apparent biases. Otherwise no sane mind can believe that NCBC report was something which can be considered as a fair report and need legal support.

While the actual bias of the NCBC and the interests of OBC communities is clearly visible from the analysis of the NCBC report done. The only thing which is left in the exercise is the identification of the apparent bias and for that we need to identify the degree of suspicion which would provide the grounds on which a decision should be set aside for apparent bias.

To identify that degree of suspicion we have two tests, as:

a) real likelihood of bias, and

b) Reasonable suspicion of bias.

For identifying the real likelihood of bias we need to identify- whether the facts, as assessed by the court, give rise to a real likelihood of bias. In *R v Gough* (1993), the House of Lords chose to state the test in terms of a "real danger of bias", and emphasized that the test was concerned with the possibility, not probability, of bias. Lord Goff of Chieveley also stated that "the court should look at the matter through the eyes of a reasonable man, because the court in cases such as these personifies the reasonable man".

However, some Commonwealth jurisdictions disapproved this test because of criticisms like the high emphasis on the court's view of the facts gives insufficient emphasis to the perception of the public. The tool used by the forces of Adharma to avoid the appearance of biases in their approach.

The House of Lords in *Porter v Magill* (2001) addressed those concerns and adjusted the *Gough* test by stating it to be "whether the fair-minded and informed observer, having considered the facts, would conclude that there was a real possibility that the tribunal was biased". So, at present we have this test in the UK from where Indian judiciary traces its origin.

The second test of reasonable suspicion test, was defined by Singapore courts as, "whether a reasonable and fair-minded person sitting in court and knowing all the relevant facts would have a reasonable suspicion that a fair trial for the litigant is not possible."

*While a reasonable and fair-minded person doesn't have the privilege to sit in the court and identify the bias now, But I hope that the above exercise on NCBC report has clearly displayed to a reasonable and fair-minded people that how much biased the whole reports was which Supreme Court made as binding for Government.*

ॐ 6

## Jat Reservation and the Pathetic Media

How Bogus Media Tries to Manipulate Opinions

The most important thing to withstand Adharma and promote Dharma is to be aware of the Dharma. When you are aware of Dharma you know how I need to look at the arguments given by Adharma and what I'm supposed to do. But this little thing is very difficult to do. Our immediate pleasures and lack of enthusiasm towards hard work and self evaluation of objects or happenings makes it easy for the forces of Adharma to create spells and circulate false propaganda as truth.

When they have little substance in their arguments or views they will try to play around one thing while giving little or no information about the other perspective. They will shout like dog to ignite the passions of people. Because our passion makes it difficult for us to keep calm and behave what we are. In the war against Ravana, Asura tried it many times and Laxman feel into their trap at times, but the guidance from Lord Ram helped him in controlling those passions and showing the Asura what it means to be an Arya.

## Introduction

The most important and the last tool of the forces of Adharma is spread of falsehood. Today media is the medium through which they will spread lies, create fears in the mind of people or promote a specific kind of ideology to ignite the passions in the people.

E.g. it is known to everyone in India that how much successful woman from Haryana and Jat community are in sports in comparison to the rest of India. But people are forced to believe that it is only Khaps and Patriarchy which is stopping the girls. No person is allowed to apply his/her mind by them to discover the real truth.

Similarly, the media and courts in cohesion, which is now joined by activists and NGOs will tell that Khaps are reasons for the increase in crime against women while they will sit on the pile of cases, news items where woman was killed because of not accepting someone proposals or acid was thrown on her.

They will just arouse the passions of people to keep them away from proper analysis of crimes and criminals, because if you do that you will understand about Dharma and their temptations will stop working on you. This will end the market of their falsehoods, as you have stopped accepting those falsehoods as the truth.

## How they spread falsehood

Let's look at some of the articles written on Jat Reservation and my observations on the same in Italic.

*The first is this lady named Nilanjana Mukherjee, who has given a heading to ignite the passions at very first instance. But when you look at the article you will find that she has nothing objective to substantiate her claims except same old vague things that Jat's can't have reservation under Article 15 (4) and 16 (4) (with no mention of the articles), which I will answer in the end.*

*The level of her knowledge and the website can be gauged from the fact that when I told the India Legal Live that the knowledge of your reporter is visible from the fact that she can't pick the names right from the things in front, how can she pick the Articles right. I want to write a counter article to the same. Instead of that they tried to correct the name and even after that they left one mistake.*

**Special Report by India Legal Live**

**Jat Reservation: Flexing Their Muscles**       **March 31, 2018**

**Despite various governments succumbing to pressure tactics by this affluent community to be included in the central list of OBCs, the apex court has shot it down**

~By Nilanjana Mukherjee

Jats in various states have often flexed their muscles, demanding to be included in the Backward Classes list. Pitched battles, torching of vehicles and other forms of aggression have been part of this agitation. However, the Supreme Court has not given in and included them in the list.

In fact, recently, there was a miscellaneous application relating to Jat reservation which came up in the Supreme Court in *Subhash Chandra Gahlwat v. Union Of India*. The matter was dismissed by the apex court.

This demand of the Jats has had a long history. In 2015, the Supreme Court in Ram Singh v. Union of India overruled the Union government's notification of March 4, 2014, for providing reservations to the Jat community in nine states by including them in the central list of Other Backward Classes. The decision came as a response to numerous petitions demanding reservation in 1997. After receiving these petitions, the National Commission for Backward Classes (NCBC) conducted a study and submitted a report on November 28, 1997, in which it recommended inclusion only of Jats from Rajasthan, except Bharatpur and Dholpur districts.

Another meeting was held by the NCBC on June 20, 2011, after it received many representations from the Jat community to review its earlier report. Thereafter, on July 19, 2011, the NCBC approached the Indian Council of Social Science Research (ICSSR) to again conduct a survey.

Meanwhile, the Prime Minister's Office wrote a letter on June 4, 2013, to the ministry of social justice and empowerment, saying a decision had been taken to constitute a Group of Ministers (GoM) to interact with Jat representatives and discuss their demand. The GoM met on two occasions—October 28, 2013, and October 30, 2013.

## SAMPLE SURVEY

The first request it put forward was that the NCBC reconsider its earlier decision of conducting the sample survey and tender its advice on the basis of material already available. The second was that the survey work, which had already begun in Gujarat, be restricted to the confirmed list of Jat variants and on the basis of these results, the ICSSR and NCBC would tender their advice.

Thereafter, the cabinet decided to request the NCBC to go ahead with the first option—to tender its advice based on existing material. The cabinet further said that Bihar, Uttarakhand and the NCT of Delhi also be included in the reference given to NCBC. Finally, on February 26, 2014, the NCBC submitted its advice, stating that the Jat community had not met the criteria for inclusion in the central list of OBCs. It said that merely belonging to an agricultural community could not give it the status of backward class. The NCBC found that Jats were not socially or educationally backward and suggested non-caste based identification of backward classes.

This finding was criticised by the cabinet which did not accept it. It then resolved to include Jats in the central list of Other Backward Classes for Bihar, Gujarat, Haryana, Himachal Pradesh, the NCT of Delhi, Bharatpur and Dholpur districts of Rajasthan, Uttar Pradesh and Uttarakhand. This impugned notification was issued on March 4, 2014.

# NO DISCRIMINATION

While deciding this case, the Supreme Court referred to several constitutional and statutory provisions such as Article 15 which prohibits discrimination on the ground of religion, race, caste, sex or place of birth. Clause (4) of Article 15 provides that "nothing in this article or in clause (2) of article 29 shall prevent the State from making any special provision for the advancement of any socially and educationally backward classes of citizens or for the Scheduled Castes and the Scheduled Tribes". Article 16 provides for equality of opportunity in matters of public employment in Clause (4) thereof that "nothing in this article shall prevent the State from making any provision for the reservation of appointments or posts in favour of any backward class of citizens which, in the opinion of the State, is not adequately represented in the services under the State". Reference was also made to Articles 38, 46 and 340.

The Bench laid stress on the judgement in *Indra Sawhney & Ors. v. UOI & Ors* which saw the necessity for establishment of a permanent/specialised body to which complaints of non-inclusion or wrong inclusion of groups, classes and sections in the list of OBCs can be made from time to time. This led to the establishment of the NCBC Act.

Backwardness is a manifestation caused by several circumstances which may be social, cultural, economic, educational or even political. Owing to historical conditions, particularly in Hindu society, recognition of backwardness has been associated with caste. The Court said that though caste may be a prominent and distinguishing factor for easy determination of backwardness of a social group, it has been routinely discouraging the identification of a group as backward solely on the basis of caste.

# BENCH OPINION

The Bench finally held: "The perception of a self-proclaimed socially backward class of citizens or even the perception of the advanced classes as to the social status of the less fortunates cannot continue to be a constitutionally permissible yardstick for determination of backwardness, both in the context of Articles 15(4) and 16(4) of the Constitution. Neither can any longer backwardness be a matter of determination on the basis of mathematical formulae evolved by taking into account social, economic and educational indicators. Determination of backwardness must also cease to be relative; possible wrong inclusions cannot be the basis for further inclusions but the gates would be opened only to permit entry of the most distressed. Any other inclusion would be a serious abdication of the constitutional duty of the State. Judged by the aforesaid standards we must hold that inclusion of the politically organised classes (such as Jats) in the list of backward classes mainly, if not solely, on the basis that on same parameters other groups who have fared better have been so included cannot be affirmed. We cannot agree with the view taken by the Union Government that Jats in the 9 (nine) States in question is a backward community so as to be entitled to inclusion in the Central Lists of Other Backward Classes for the States concerned. The view taken by the NCBC to the contrary is adequately supported by good and acceptable reasons which furnished a sound and reasonable basis for further consequential action on the part of the Union

Government. In the above situation we cannot hold the notification dated 4.3.2014 to be justified. Accordingly the aforesaid notification bearing No. 63 dated 4.3.2014 including the Jats in the Central List of Other Backward Classes for the States of Bihar, Gujarat, Haryana, Himachal Pradesh, Madhya Pradesh, NCT of Delhi, Bharatpur and Dholpur Districts of Rajasthan, Uttar Pradesh and Uttarakhand is set aside and quashed."

Thus, the Supreme Court rejected the notification which tried to include Jats in the central list of OBCs.


My Observations:
- *Someone should ask this lady that does she know that before Article 15 (4) and 16 (4) we have Article 14 which provides Equality before Law. When and where NCBC and Supreme Court has shown even a scant regard to that in the whole exercise.*
- *Even if we go by Article 15 (4) and 16 (4), when and where NCBC or Supreme Court has shown any fact, data or statistic to show that their observations are true in accordance to those articles.*
- *When you don't have anything to prove your points, you resort to the tactics used by NCBC and Supreme Court and that is to speak a lot with nothing to support that. It is a kind of Social Proofing mechanism which we see in advertisements where brands like Coalgate, Bournvita etc. will show a person as doctor or expert to stop your research on the whole thing.*
- *While the whole article is as worthy as the knowledge of this lady but if I will say more on that, these frivolous mentality people will project it is as patriarchy.*


*The second article in this list is this article by Vipul Mudgal, who is Director and Chief Executive of Common Cause. He also heads the Inclusive Media for Change project at CSDS (Centre for Study of Developing Societies). Let's look at his opinions before knowing the truth behind them.*


## The Absurdity of Jat Reservation

Rather than recklessly expanding the beneficiary, what is needed is to address India's economic stagnation and removing weaknesses in reservations.

When the Gujjars blocked the national highways around Delhi, people wanted to know their story. Their dismal condition evoked a grudging sympathy, more so in contrast with their Meena neighbors who had the scheduled tribe tag. But a similar belligerence by the Jat community has met with shock and disbelief. It is plain absurd that a community that dominates every sphere of a state's life should cry discrimination.

Albert Camus describes absurdity as something that appears illogical but not logically impossible. For instance, absurdity strikes you in the face when the supposed victims of economic hardship use expensive SUVs to block roads in Gurgaon! So will it be absurd by the same logic if the Brahmins start believing that they are victims of the Varna system? Or will it be absurd if the Rajputs of Rajasthan declare a war on New Delhi because some of them feel they are being pushed around?

For the record, a section of Rajasthan's Rajputs have been at war for over a decade with tacit support coming from all political parties. And for years the Brahmins in North India, Gujarat and Kerala have been demanding reservation on count of discrimination. Rajputs and Brahmins, the original tormentors in the Varna system, have joined hands to form a Social Justice Front in Rajasthan. In Punjab, some Brahmins have formed a self-styled Parshuram Sena, which stands up for their oppressed brethren!

Fortunately for now, talks with the Jats have started in Haryana after 11 deaths and injuries to 150 people, although the barricades have not been lifted everywhere. The agitating Jats have been promised a favourable bill in the next assembly session. The neighbouring Rajasthan already has reservation for Jats under the other backward class (OBC) category, but the National Commission for Backward Classes (NCBC) denied similar claims of backwardness to Jats in Haryana, Uttar Pradesh, Madhya Pradesh and Delhi. The Supreme Court too rejected their claims on the central OBC list. But, what legal battles could not get them in years was almost yielded in less than ten days of violence and mayhem.

The most shocking thing about the agitation is the degree of aggression on display and the spontaneity of its spread. India is no stranger to destruction of public property during protests but it takes a dominant caste to burn down police posts and railway stations, cut off water supply to the capital, and block the army vehicles. Even a martyr's body (also a Jat) could not be taken home and had to be flown in.

## The politics of reservation

Jats are to Haryana what the Patels are to Gujarat, the Rajputs to Rajasthan and the Marathas to Maharashtra – the dominant castes, without a doubt. Some of them are poor but most possess land, cattle, businesses, muscle power or political clout. What is common between all these peasant castes – and many others in North India such as Lodhs, Kurmis, Yadavs and Koeries – is that their landholding is fragmenting fast. Having prospered after the green revolution, these castes are now facing agrarian distress and deep stagnation in the rural economy. Two successive droughts and untimely rains have worsened the crisis. Their anxieties are real, never mind the absurdity of their situation.

According to the National Sample Survey (NSS 59th round), the average land holding in India came down from 2.63 acres in 1960-61 to 1.06 acres in 2003-4, or about 60% in four decades. A CSDS study of the farmers in 18 states of India has confirmed the NSS findings that given the choice, a substantial number of farmers would prefer to do something else. For the peasant castes the easiest way out of this predicament is an urban job, preferably in the police or the army.

The implementation of the Mandal Commission report in 1989 benefited some peasant communities at the cost of many others. But once it happened, no politician or party was able to counter it. Even those who cried foul and challenged Prime Minister V P Singh, its architect, were forced to eat their words. Ten years later the game was upped by the first BJP prime minister, Atal Bihari Vajpayee, when he announced reservation for the Jats on the eve of elections in three north Indian states, including in Rajasthan where he made the announcement at an election rally.

Following this, the NCBC issued a notification to include Rajasthan's Jat community among backward castes, with the exception of those from the erstwhile princely states of Bharatpur and Dholpur. The commission is said to have made a grave mistake: it used 1931 Census figures to gauge backwardness of a community without factoring the rise of agricultural communities after the post-independence expansion of irrigation.

Grievances over reservations existed before Mandal but they did not lead to serious conflicts or turmoil. There was also the realisation that its net effect was more integrative than subversive and that it empowered the poorest. But Mandal brought in its wake, besides a new breed of identity politics, a spate of violence and unrest which keeps recurring at an alarming frequency. It also opened a Pandora's box of new set of demands coming from hitherto unknown or unpredicted sections, of which there are thousands in India.

But in spite of all its traction, the OBC politics did not help Singh come back to power. Vajpayee's election eve bonanza to Jats too failed to yield desired results for the BJP in 1999 and the extension of the same did not benefit the Congress in 2014. In Rajasthan the Jat reservation created new imbalances for the other OBC communities and in many competitive exams the better educated and prosperous Jats cornered two third of all seats, general and OBC. It is worrying that the obvious lesson for other peasant communities is to assert and prevail wherever they have the numbers.

What is so absurd about knee-jerk legislations is that rather than providing comfort to the poorer OBCs with little assets, it forces them to compete against their powerful neighbours. A rational answer lies more in addressing rural India's economic stagnation and removing weaknesses in reservations through consensus rather than recklessly expanding the list of beneficiaries. It also puts the whole idea of reservations on its head. The founding fathers of the Constitution had dreamt that the ultimate aim of the job reservations was to annihilate the caste system. But the post-Mandal politics ended up nurturing the curse of caste by rousing a hysterical politicisation of all caste groups.

*My Observations:*

- *While the person has claimed that the CSDS has done study but he has nothing to show from that. What he tries to do through all those words is to talk and talk with no data, fact or thing to substantiate his claim of absurdity.*

- *Add to that instead of talking about Jats he takes the article to other direction and talks about Rajput, Brahmin Varna etc. with no knowledge of what Varna actually means or having groups is very common. E.g. in the previous chapter I added images from the representations against Jat Reservation. In that almost all the person belonged to some organization created in the name of caste or overall OBC interest.*

- *The depth of his studies or understanding can be gauged from the fact that while he found one SUV used to stop the roads (that too with no substance) but had no understanding about the thousands of protesters who travelled on others tractor-trolley for protests or people from villages who gathered in large in Rohtak.*

- *Every year around 2crore two-wheelers and 20-25lakh are sold in India. In that if someone used one vehicle what does it signify? To me one sporadic incident signifies nothing. As the person is from CSDS, he should know that there is something called empirical study also. Do that, it will serve you and your organization better.*

- *In reality, he represents those foolish people who are happy to have people get identified by their profession, ideology or any other identity except the biological identity of Jati.*

While sitting in the comfort of your home just analyze yourself. You are 50% what your father is and 50 % of what your mother is. You are 25% of your grandparents from both sides. You are 12.5% of what your great grandparents were.

If I talk about myself, my father belonged to 1 Jat Gotra and my Mother belonged to another Jat Gotra. My grandmother had 3rd Gotra and maternal grandmother had another. My great grandmother and great maternal grandmother had other Jat Gotra. So, when I identify myself as Jat what is wrong in that? It is the foundation of me and irrespective of profession, ideology (which is not natural and can change easily) it will remain the same.

## Article 15 and 16 of the Constitution

From media to the representations against the Jat reservation we find that people try to claim that Article 15 (4) and 16 (4) of the Indian Constitution restrict the reservation for Jats. So let's have a reading of those articles and identify whether the conclusions taken by them are valid or just the figments of imagination as we observed in the rest of things.

- The **Article 15** of our Constitution says:

*Prohibition of discrimination on grounds of religion, race, caste, sex or place of birth*

(1) The State shall not discriminate against any citizen on grounds only of religion, race, caste, sex, place of birth or any of them

(2) No citizen shall, on grounds only of religion, race, caste, sex, place of birth or any of them, be subject to any disability, liability, restriction or condition with regard to

(a) access to shops, public restaurants, hotels and palaces of public entertainment; or

(b) the use of wells, tanks, bathing ghats, roads and places of public resort maintained wholly or partly out of State funds or dedicated to the use of the general public

(3) Nothing in this article shall prevent the State from making any special provision for women and children

(4) Nothing in this article or in clause ( 2 ) of Article 29 shall prevent the State from making any special provision for the advancement of any socially and educationally backward classes of citizens or for the Scheduled Castes and the Scheduled Tribes.

- The **Article 16** of our Constitution says:

*Equality of opportunity in matters of public employment*

(1) There shall be equality of opportunity for all citizens in matters relating to employment or appointment to any office under the State

(2) No citizen shall, on grounds only of religion, race, caste, sex, descent, place of birth, residence or any of them, be ineligible for, or discriminated against in respect or, any employment or office under the State

(3) Nothing in this article shall prevent Parliament from making any law prescribing, in regard to a class or classes of employment or appointment to an office under the Government of, or any local or other authority within, a State or Union territory, any requirement as to residence within that State or Union territory prior to such employment or appointment

(4) Nothing in this article shall prevent the State from making any provision for the reservation of appointments or posts in favor of any backward class of citizens which, in the opinion of the State, is not adequately represented in the services under the State

(5) Nothing in this article shall affect the operation of any law which provides that the incumbent of an office in connection with the affairs of any religious or denominational institution or any member of the governing body thereof shall be a person professing a particular religion or belonging to a particular denomination.

*So, the first thing from the articles is that the meaning of State includes the government not the NCBC. The opinion of the Government of India is known to everyone. Still they are trying to impose the opinion of NCBC as the opinion of State.*

*Secondly, we have seen from the NCBC report that how it tried to manipulate the educational backwardness of Jats as because of economic soundness. This argument is given by NCBC to avoid the application of 15 (4). If we accept this vague argument for a moment than it means that as a community Jats are the people who like to live with ease instead of doing hard work.*

*But when NCBC and other people are required to avoid the application of 16 (4), they will say that if reservation is given to them they will garner the maximum benefit.*

*One side NCBC claims that Jat as a person doesn't like to study, as when they have money they dropout from school in comparison to others who are forced to drop because of money. But on other side NCBC is saying that if reservation is given to Jat they will garner the maximum benefit from reservation.*

*Only a biased person can accept both of these arguments despite being the opposite in nature. A rational person will always ask -what kind of picture you want to paint about Jat. First, be sure what you want to show. Whether the community is hard working or comfort loving? If they don't want to study then how come they will take the benefits from you.*

ॐ 7

## The Added Responsibilities on Court

**E**nding the **I**ntrigue **W**ork **against** **D**harma

While in theory we have expanded the principle of Natural Justice by adding the third principle to it as: The order which is passed affecting the rights of an individual must be a speaking order. A speaking order helps in excluding the possibility of arbitrariness in the action. A speaking order helps in furtherance of achieving the end where society is governed by Rule of law.

But instead of all those noble considerations we had a order which was more of a bald order with no reason to support it. To cover that bald order, the forces of Adharma used every arbitrary and irresponsible criteria or arguments they can use. But the most unfortunate thing is that the highest court of India with the responsibility of "Yato-Dharmasto-Jaya" protected those activities of Adharma.

## Introduction

The way we think, perceive things or events around us depends on the kind of education we have. Our education helps us to understand things around us and derive conclusions from it. That understanding of our surroundings guides our behavior and actions.

For immediate creation of a society governed by Rule of Law we have developed certain conventions, principles and laws to be followed. But because of personal biases, interests or thoughts people tend to move towards Adharma, forgetting that the will of God is expressed through those laws of nature.

If someone wants to work for Dharma, he/she needs to first understand about the laws of nature. That understanding of the laws of nature will help him in respecting the diversity on land and work towards the continuity of that.

## The Education and Surroundings

The education of a person guides his/her perceptions on the surroundings. If we have an education which tells us that it is good to keep the society together we will try to join people. If we have an education which is to break the society we will act as a disruptive force.

Similarly, if we have an education where people are told to secure maximum benefits for themselves and relatives they will keep that as goal. But if we have people with education on Dharma we will have people like Lord Ram who sacrificed personal benefits for the larger good.

The nature made groupings at species (Prajati) and subspecies (Jati) level based on biology to help in the evolution on earth. But the people on earth divided themselves into many groups based on profession, lifestyle and other social factors.

It is these social factors which force people in neglecting the interests of other groups. When we overcome those social considerations and value only the biological differences we understand the meaning of life and the importance of nature. The meaning of life, which helps us in development and propagation of ideas which speak for themselves under all situations.

## The meaning of a speaking order

In Law also we have something called as a speaking order. A Speaking order is an order where the party, against whom an order is passed, in fair play, must know the reasons of passing the order. It helps the party to know the reasons for having an order against its interests.

In Writ Petition Civil 274 of 2014 we have seen how the principles of natural justice were violated. The impact of that bald order was that to demonstrate the errors of that order I was forced to work out on the report used for that order rather than the judgment alone.

The personal ideologies make a judge as much a counsel to the case as being the adjudicator. But instead of avoiding and keeping those tendencies to a bare minimum some judges have worked hard to increase and preserve it. These ideologies have influenced the courts so much that they aren't even ready to listen against that.

The institutions which are made to protect a moral attitude are going against that moral attitude because of control by those ideologies. The media is trying to cash those ideologies by spreading lies and fears among people on challenges to those ideologies.

*But the illogical and irrational ideas of the report are enough to show that the foundation on which the judgment is based has no ground under them. Because of these weak foundations I'm able to demonstrate the errors of the whole exercise despite having a bald order on the case.*

*Now it is an added responsibility on the court to reverse those decisions, as the support for Adharma is so deep in those structures that people are forced to work outside. It is that Adharma that because of which the right of appeal has become a mercy plea.*

*I hope and wish that with a unanimous concurrence the judges should work on it. It is an important decision and it should have a nonpartisan approach, not an actual and apparent bias. It should be according to the legal public expectations and the conventions, not a discreet exercise. Most importantly, it should be based on established and true facts instead of assumed historical facts with assumed representations in support of that.*

*The reservation was ordained and established by the people of India with the hope that it will serve the people who need it, not the people who misuse it. It is a help to the people not a right given to the existing communities to define and mould it as per own conditions, tastes or benefits.*

*Once again* in words of **Justice Douglas**, "Law has reached its finest moments when it has freed man from the unlimited discretion of some ruler, some civil or military official, some bureaucrat. Where discretion, is absolute, man has always suffered. At times, it has been his property that has been invaded; at times, his privacy; at times, his liberty of movement; at times, his freedom of thought; at times, his life. Absolute discretion is a ruthless master. It is more destructive of freedom than any of man's other inventions."

# Epilogue

Adharma on earth has spread so much that soon we will need a combination of all the powers on earth to live by Dharma. As, to have balance in our thoughts, aspirations, philosophies and actions we need Dharma as an essential consideration, as

- Dharma brings the gods will in our actions,
- Dharma makes the protection of nature part of our actions, and
- Dharma removes the ills from the earth, bringing continuity of life.

Therefore, in order to spread that Dharma I'm required to explain about Dharma (the second part of the **Yato-Dharmasto-Jaya**).

Dharma explains the laws of nature to us. The Laws of nature which acts as part of our life. The laws which comes out even if bolted behind a door with hundred different locks with hundred different locations of the keys. The laws which have remained unchanged from the start of life on earth and will remain the same till the end of life, irrespective of any kingdom, phylum or even subspecies under consideration.

Today, we have people who give decisions against them to excite hatred and disgust towards the laws of nature. The scholars and media project them as unscientific and parochial thoughts to rob the people from having curiosity and sympathy towards them. Many religious and political leaders deny the existence of them to keep the people depended on them.

But these laws of nature are the basis on which things happen for an Arya. The sooner we learn them, the better will be our actions. Thousands of years ago Lord Ram learned those laws from the Great Saptarishis (Sages) and worked on spreading those laws across the life and breadth of people.

I hope and pray that if not the same extent, at least to a part of that extent I will also be successful to spread them under the guidance of Lord Ram, Mata Sita and My Deity. I wish good luck to all and hope that soon I will be ready with the second part of the book to spread the message of Dharma, helping in the establishment of Dharma.